T0365907

LOST

JOHNATHON LOUGHRY

ARCHWAY
PUBLISHING

Archway Publishing books may be ordered through booksellers or by contacting:

Archway Publishing
1663 Liberty Drive
Bloomington, IN 47403
www.archwaypublishing.com
844-669-3957

ISBN: 978-1-6657-4080-7 (sc)
ISBN: 978-1-6657-4081-4 (e)

Library of Congress Control Number: 2023905114

Print information available on the last page.

Archway Publishing rev. date: 03/21/2023

CONTENTS

THE BEGINNING

I have a story here that will bring People to tears, hurt some, and open the eyes of many I believe. It is known as My life.

From the time I was a small Child My life was either grand or desperate, that is a fact. The life I have lived since June 1st 1960 has been an incredible run. It has been filled with true love yet at the same time it has been a heart broken miserable existence.

What I am going to put down in writing is going to be very hard to believe I completely understand. But I will speak only the truth. All I have to say here is from the memories I have had from the age of two up to the moment of writing this.

I have a couple of things I hope to achieve by writing My life story. Of course one is to prosper. I have been a construction worker for well over forty years and I am tired. I have no real retirement to speak of, I have wasted My money as a Fool is known to do. Another thing I hope to achieve is to awaken Lives to ways of the World that I feel They need to see. For some it can be enlightening on how some People fall apart. For others it may just be what They need to lead Them down a proper path in life.

I hope You will read this with an open mind and see My plight in life. I was destined to fail, and what I have been through is excruciating. Sympathy is not what I seek at all, I really just want out of this miserable life I have known.

One thing You need to understand is My Family has a history of retardation. That will explain a lot. I sincerely have great hopes that My story will help change many lost Lives.

THE START

How to tell a story such as Mine? Do You start with the very first part or jump ahead and then come back?

The first part of My life I actually look like a Winner, the second part I come off as a " Real Winner " as People say.

To keep from becoming confused I better start from the beginning.

Well here We go.

My first actual thought in life that I can remember? It was My second birthday. My Grandparents on My Dads side gave Me a Puppy for My birthday. I don't even remember playing with the damn thing. The next memory of that Pooch was when Dad told Me to go feed My Dog. When I went outside with the food He lunged at Me, He wasn't playing and He had grown some. He was on a chain so I was safe. Dad soon took Him hunting, as Dad told Me when I asked about the Pup years later, He said the Dog saw the gun and ran away.

That in itself will enlighten You on how My story will unfold.

It was around that same time I was in the kitchen when Dad brought in a quarter of Deer. I remember I looked up as He tossed it on the table. Poached was the word He used. There was a blood red air about Him too. When He saw Me standing there We both stood and looked at each other in shock.

With My Family I can say here and now He will deny it. I have confronted Him and Mom on the things They have tried to make Me look bad with. Mom told Me once, this was years after what I am speaking of though, that the Prison here in (a town in a cold state) was allowing Prisoners to go to town and rape Women. It came back when I was near heat stroke on a roof and when I saw Her that day I asked about it, She denied ever saying such. A few weeks later Dad told Me the same damn thing. I am not so gullible as I once was. At the time I was first told I let it roll off My back. Now I despise such crap.

Back to where I began.

It was around that same time, speaking of the red air and the Pup, that I learned how to climb. There was a ladder leaning against the fence. It would have been a three foot chain link, it had a ladder extending in length the height of the fence. I started to climb it. Jeffery was the neighbor Kid I ran with, He told Me not to climb it. Well, I remember starting to climb the ladder. My next memory was getting told My jacket saved My life.

Now being sixty two and living a few years in (a cold state) I look back on the jacket part, it was fall. I was told there was water in the ditch, in the fall? Not likely.

The one part that really messes with My life from that fall is that I was two years old. A two year old taking a six foot fall and hitting His head, even on dirt, had to have an impact on His thinking. The later years of My life will make a lot of sense, it makes Me realize why I have lived the disastrous life I have witnessed.

So hold onto Your hats Folks, things are about to get wild.

THE MAN CHILD

While I was still two years old the Folks decided to move Us out of (a very cold place). We landed in (a new place), in the heart of (can't say) County.

It was there that My life really took a turn. At first it was an average childhood, but after less than a year there I witnessed so much in a few months span I still have to look at it and ask if what I saw was reality. What I saw though tells Me it was in fact reality.

This is the hardest part of My life to explain. Even though the past forty years were so rough I have attempted suicide numerous times. Yet I must go on, with My life and My story.

As I say, the first part of My life in (the new place) was just life as a Child. Then one morning My life changed, for the better I believe. We were not People that could afford luxurious toys for the Children. I was sent outside to play. I now see it as a set up, there was a mud puddle. It was near the side of the yard, in a hole made in the grass. That is where I spent My days.

Now I have to state here that I believe in mental telepathy. For one reason mainly is due to what I have to say here.

One morning while playing alone, as I did everyday, I saw something. It was a Person. Yes it was a Human in My mind. I completely understand what this sounds like, and no I am not totally insane.

It is impossible to remember the first thing I heard then, but I learned so much it's amazing.

I will start by mentioning a few. "That old Boy grew", "That old Girl grew", "That old Gentleman grew", "God Damn Kids!", "Full Grown Maturity", "That Man's a Kid", "Snot nosed Kid", "Smart allecky Kid", "A lonely Boy", "A lonely Man", "What are You a Queer? No! Then take it like a Man", "Shocks the Children", "The shocking Kid", "I demand respect", "A Gentleman doesn't kiss and tell", "A Lady is discreet", Fuck You", and I never heard that one before seriously.

Yes, that is what I learned at three years old. I was playing in the mud and making mud pies. Everyday I would put them on the Neighbors fence posts, the next day I would come out and inspect them. After looking them over I would crush them and do it again. I do believe that is what caused My first fight.

The Kid next door came out one day, it was His fence. He confronted Me, not about the mud though. I feel the Kid next door was told to go and get in a fight, He picked Me.

Poor Guy started calling Me names when I acted cowardly, I told Him name calling was immature. He started screaming at Me "(My name) Belly! (My name) Belly!" and charged Me. Mistake one with (My name) Belly, I snap kicked Him in the nose. He ran home with Me right behind Him I was so shocked. His Mom yelled at Me and the rest is black. You hemorrhage to death within four hours I know now. I never even heard the word karate at the time. Ray will come back into the story a time or two later, He turned out to be a Friend You can rely on.

Back to what I was witnessing via the mind. "Name calling is childish and immature, and that is a fact of life", "You still want to be called one huh?", "Face up to the facts of life", " I am lost without You", "She looked at Me all googilly eyed", "Childish nonsense", "Wet behind the ears little Girl", "I am an Idiot", "The Kid's an Idiot", "I am a Fool", "Damn fool Kid", "Tell"em to go to Hell", that's My favorite. "It's a Man's World", "Take it like a Man"," "Good for nothing Kid", "Are You calling Me a Liar?".

I understand that this is a lot to digest, but I look at it daily and see it clear. I will continue. "The mind is a terrible thing to waste", "Are You a Man? Yes I am a Man", "We can be Men about this", "Girly", "That's a Girl if I've ever seen one", "Stop trying to be Men", "A wise Man doesn't mess with the insane", "Lost and lonely", "Loneliness is enough to drive You insane".

Believe Me I am putting a lot of thought into these words as I am writing, I sincerely do not want to say something I may have learned at a later date. During My life I have learned so much I will continue later in the book about the rest of My shocking lessons.

The list goes on. "It's a cruel World", "That's the American way", "Men!" some young Girl shrieked. "There are some things a Man just doesn't do", "Boys will be Boys", "Don't insult My intelligence", "Don't patronize Me", "It's all part of growing up", "Too cool", "Hot shot Kid", "Don't argue with Me like a Child", "Mock My words it's Childsplay" and not mark My words either. "Mockery is childsplay", "Get the Hell out of My life", "Proper Adults", "When You're in love that's all You can think about", "Those are fighting words", "Ahdult" and I purposely put the H in to get the pronunciation correct. "Real Men don't laugh", "It's not a laughing matter", "I don't claim to be something I'm not", "It's all in Your mind", "I'll wipe that smile off Your face", "Don't smile when You say that", "It's not something You can just turn off", "Silly Boy", "Take a good hard look at Yourself", "Smart ass Kid", "A Man has his wits about Him", "A Man has a certain air about Him", "Hey Kid, what's going on?", "I sure have a lot of growing up to do", "You're never as grown as You think You are", "Excitable Boy", "I was stripped of My pride, stripped of My manhood", "Can't You tell the Boy's love struck",

"There are too many Kids to cope with", "Don't stare Children it's rude", "There's a Man", "I was a womanizer", "Don't undress Me with Your mind", "I'm wise to the ways of the World", "What? You've never seen a Man before?", "What's the matter? You can't be called a Kid anymore?". I am sure there is more, for the past few days I have been adding in when I remember a new one. Now I know this is a lot to absorb, but I really was three years old and watching all of this take place. I am pretty sure there is one or two I have forgotten, but I have already put enough out there to make a head spin I am sure.

One day while I was squatting down in the mud puddle a young Man caught My attention. He was mad as hell and looking at these Boys looking at this one Person, the one that started it all. He was the same one that said He was a Fool. It actually was the same Human I saw a lot too. I looked at this angry Fella and then looked at what He was glaring at. All of these Boys that were looking at this Fool looked at Me when I said I was just a little Boy, which is one thing I had told Myself numerous times in the months preceding. When They looked at Me I stood as a Grown Man. The words were there right next to me, FULL GROWN MAN. All of Us did the same thing simultaneously, everyone of us looked at the words beside Me and then back at each other. Every damn one of them turned away and said to Themselves "We are not Men". That was the last day I saw any of those Gentlemen too.

During this time of watching these People I had the opportunity to see what Grown Adults actually feel like. I had seen a couple with the words as I did that day as well, but not one felt the exact feeling I felt when they stood. Believe Me when I say there are different types of Men. The thing is, They are all Grown. I even saw some Men that just stood off and watched. I look for the same type of Men today and have a rough time finding Them. You must realize these Men were old Gentlemen in 1963, meaning these old Farts were around at the turn of the century, They were old enough to be Children when Butch Cassidy was running around. I watched Them with real interest too. And a Grown Woman has a special feeling that is rare as well. I have seen it in a young Woman I know around eleven years ago too.

Because of what I have lived through and experienced in My life I know better than to call Myself a Grown Man. I do not to this day live as one and that I will explain a bit more later on in My story. I hope You hold on and see it through, it has been one hell of a ride.

I can see where this would sound like a wild imagination, but what I witnessed at three actually opened

My mind. I am the type that would welcome a truth serum in fact. I cannot lie to You about My life, seriously.

That was the easiest part of my life if You believe it. From here on it turns real ugly.

As far as the things I have written in this era, I understand they are unspeakable. No Man is going to admit to seeing People in his mind, They would try to commit the Boy. But I need a way out of a rough life. Also, I just might teach a Kid or two. That is My main concern here.

SCHOOL BOY YEARS

What I went through before school I actually locked away for nearly two decades. As soon as those Boys grew up I never thought of Them again. Seriously, not until My twenties, then it came flooding back. But that is a totally different story.

One thing that happened right after that look was a Christmas present. I was given a toy gun and holster, a really nice set too. I practiced everyday on My quick draw. The Kid next door and His sister were in the garage when I got My hand stuck in the garage door spring. After that I practiced left handed. I really must have been getting fast, My Parents took it away from Me. I even asked My sister to get it out of the closet for Me, She said no. That in itself tells how My Parents were. They get colder too.

My first day of school? Here is this little Man being taken to His first day of Kindergarten, I cried. Not very manly I admit. Mom still gives Me grief over it. When She came to pick Me up I didn't want to leave as She tells it.

One memory from those years was when I walked home and got My bike and rode it back to school, I wasn't supposed to in the grade I was in. Not sure, but I think it was first grade. Kindergarten was a half day so I am sure it wasn't then.

Other than that My first few years were uneventful. Up until the third grade I just remember going to school. One day I was getting ready to get in line to go back to class when I saw a Guy and a Gal standing nearby. I said something to Her and He punched Me in the gut. I cowardly got up and went to the end of the line. When I think back now I really don't remember seeing either of Them in Our school before.

The manner in which I am writing this makes Me change course now and again during My story. I am adding this part after remembering something that took place around this time. We were on the playground when I saw another part of My lesson from the People in My mind. There was this young Man and all these Gals were around Him, He said "I looked at her and saw She was too good for Me, and threw Her back to the Wolves". When He was finished I turned away and said to Myself that I hadn't had sex yet and felt like another type of Man. When I looked back at the playground there was only one Child left besides Me and She was hauling ass to get out of there. Really, (not allowed) Elementary on (some street).

The next year was pretty uneventful as well. Then I got My Cowboy boots. Being a Cowboys Son I was proud of them. But after a few rains, We walked to school, they turned green. Pea green boots they were called. That and being named (My name) caused Me a lot of grief. "That's a Girls name" was a regular saying. I always looked at Them and told Myself I don't want to hurt You, fact. And I forgot all about kicking the Kid next door.

That kinda crap went on for at least two years. During that time other occurrences took place as well. There was the time I asked numerous times to go to the bathroom while in third grade class, I pissed My pants. That next summer We were in (a very cold place) when I saw My cousin in the ditch in front of Grandpa's house. When I asked Him what He was doing He said He was throwing rocks at cars, I jumped in the ditch to help. The first car We threw a rock at slammed on the brakes and backed up, We ran. He knew Grandpa. I was hiding behind a bush half My size when Grandpa came around the corner, I lit out for the house with Him kicking Me in the butt with every stride He took. I still can't believe I got the door open without Him snatching My dumbass. I streaked across the room and jumped into Dad's lap. All Dad asked was what did I do. Didn't see My cousin for the rest of the day either. That afternoon Mom had the Neighbors bring by some horses, all I could do was watch. When I asked to ride I was shut down of course. That next school year, the fourth grade, I was told to draw something. I drew something alright, it had something to do with horses. Mom was called to school, He must have a vivid imagination She said.

By the fifth grade My home life turned into a real nightmare. My oldest sister began screaming at Me everyday right after school, it was pretty much the same thing everytime too. One thing She would yell is that I had a Girlfriend, the Kid next door's Sister. I spent a lot of time at Their house, but don't really remember Her ever being real talkative. She turned out to be a good looking Woman too, We are Friends on (social media). It is no wonder I can drive through (a town in a hot state) and not even stop and visit. I always had the same reaction, I looked at Her bewildered. After listening for a while I would stomp My foot and all four Girls ran and locked Themselves in the bathroom. I then messed with Them for the longest time, I would unlock the door or stand where they couldn't see Me until They came out and hit the door. I had four Sisters and not a single Brother. Dad had already told Me what would happen if I laid hands on Them. Seriously, this took place until I was around a Sophomore in high school. It was another thing that My mind blocked out, even when it happened the next day I really didn't recall it from the day before. I did mention the fall I took at two, I really think it messed the Boy up pretty good. It doesn't help either that mental retardation runs in the Family. Dads Father was a little slow I could tell, and I have a first cousin that is severely retarded. My nephew's Son also has His bout with it.

I tell the truth when I say I thought of committing suicide in the fifth grade.

I actually hated learning as well. If a math question was 10 x 15 I would write whatever came into My mind. Needless to say I went into special education classes. Now as a Carpenter I can rattle equations off like nothing. I raced a Friends Daughter. She used a calculator and I used My brain. She finally looked at Me and said "You're fast". Let's say the problem is 35x25. 35x20=700 (35x2+70 add a 0=700) 30x5=150, and 5x5=25=175. Add them together and You have 875. You just break it down in Your head. All fractions divide in half by multiplying the denominator by two. For example ¼ split in half is ⅛, 4x2=8. 5/32 is 5/64 and so on.

Where I went to school was a Chicano neighborhood. The stories I hear about it now is the Police won't venture into there after dark. (Damn, I can't say where). The Mexicans never bothered Me in elementary school, but junior high was a different animal. I walked up to (a Kid in school) one day, I ran. He was going to beat Me with His belt buckle. On the first day of seventh grade I was robbed by a Mexican Kid at knife point. I told Him I only had a quarter and he took it. I sure as hell wasn't going to say anything, good way to get jumped, but the Kid next door was there and He blabbed it to My Mom. I was instantly put into Karate classes. I even had to point the Kid out.

The Kid next door always seemed to be around when something like that took place. There was the time My youngest sister, said the Boys down the street were bothering Her. I was on My bike and in Their backyard fast, The Kid next door was right behind me. They weren't home so nothing happened, and to be honest I never thought about it again.

I learned two more things, but this time I actually saw both People. I know it was around 1969 because We were in Our Econoline Ford van. Right on (again can't say). I caught "And then they look at You like you've lost Your mind". I looked at Him and His feeling was that burning red sensation Men have. The other one was a young Woman, and it was truly just around the corner on (nope, can't say it) that I saw Her, "I am the first one to admit to it". Both of those sayings really mean a lot to Me now.

It was around that time, give or take a year, that I almost drowned. We were at a beach when I was standing there watching the waves crash. A freak wave came up and grabbed Me. That was the last thing I remember until I was spinning in the undertow. I have only felt real fear twice in My life, that was the first. I knew I was about to drown, My lungs were burning for air. It was then that I saw the sun through the water and kicked off the ocean floor. In all reality I have done that same thing twice. In 1989 I think it was I was working across the road from the pier and went to the beach after work. No shit, almost the exact spot it happened again. There was no spinning while scared, I kicked My butt out with nothing but reflex. I really do not recall what took place under water. After the first time it happened I walked over to My family and they sat there like nothing had happened. I have written to the Lifeguards in that area too, all You have to do is kick when You see the sun through the water. Many swimmers have been dragged out to sea due to the current.

During the seventh grade I learned another saying in My mind, "I wasn't man enough to hold Her in My arms", I keep thinking there is another one too, but I can't place it right now.

Seventh grade was also when I started my Hoodlum days. The Kid across the street and another started walking to school together with Me. They started Me smoking and stealing. In eighth grade I walked with two brothers from next door, two Brothers. They were just as bad. The older Brother made sure We ran everywhere We went, trying to get the fat Kid in shape I see now. He taught me how to shoplift. And He grew some pot on the roof of Our house. He also taught Me how to huff, I don't think that did My brain any good.

It was then that I got My first job, I had mowed lawns before is all. You can't really call it a job, We sold flowers on the street corners. You met at the shop and They took You out in a van and dropped You off. $10 a day on average, I thought it was alright. I bought My first turntable and a few records then. Twice I had some Jerk walk up and grab a bunch and run off, You couldn't leave the rest or they'd all be gone likely.

I think maybe those two years could have been the reason We moved back to (a cold state) after eighth grade. I am pretty sure things would have escalated into bigger things if We stayed in (some state). We were there during the sixties, there were a lot of crazy things to see. There was the time a Cop came by telling Everyone over His PA to stay in the house. Dad called his Buddy down the street who was watching a gang fight in front of his house. The Strawberry Festival was always wild. The Folks worked the ticket booths, Dad said They watched riots almost nightly. Mom was President of the PTA and the PTA ran the booths. We were not allowed there after dark, during the day We were all over it.

Just like (a big amusement park). Dad worked for (where Dad worked) and once a year They bought out the place. We would go there and not see a single Person, really. Back then You just walked in without paying and bought tickets if You wanted to ride. We had a big stash from before We got to go for nothing. One day I asked Mom what She was going to do with them, She gave them to Me. Me and the Kid next door had a blast for a whole summer.

Dad working for (where Dad worked) had its advantages, I learned to drive at five years old. He delivered the fleet golf carts to tournaments every weekend, I was usually with Him. I drove onto the second deck of the trailer after a while. I almost killed Myself once, real close too. I was hauling ass in reverse when I saw a trailer parked behind Me, I missed the brake and gave it some gas. Dad came running around the corner when He heard the crash. Scared Me a little.

Other than having a few of the Guys trying to pick fights with me, and Me showing what a Wuss I really was, life in junior high at (My junior high school) wasn't all that much to talk about. Then We moved back to (a cold place).

(A COLD STATE) KIDS

We moved back to (a cold place) between My eighth and ninth grade in school. It didn't take long to figure out there are Bullies everywhere You go.

I was walking home one afternoon when two Boys started towards Me. They were younger, but both of Them were broad, I knew it was a fight and told Myself here We go, I was not walking away from this one. Just before either of Us could say anything a local tough Guy stepped out from behind a building. I will always respect Him for what He did. He told those two to leave Me alone, They didn't argue. It was one of those times I never saw Them before or after. I still feel it was a Family Member that set it up. Too many times has something like that happened to not believe My Family was involved.

Going back to just before school started. I was in the vice principal's office with My Mom getting registered for school. She told Him She wanted Me in some sort of athletics, I was a chubby Kid, I said alright I'll play football. Well that didn't really set well with the Players on the team, They didn't accept a slow Kid. Slow mentally and not a fast runner either. But I played for four years. By My senior year They called Me (My last name) evil eye, because I was about to explode on these little pricks due to their harassment. I tell you now, don't let Your Kids be the ones that hold it in. It is not how You want Your Children to grow up.

My highlights in football, I blocked the allstate tackle on Our last practice ever. And I made every tackle in a game that same year. On Our first day of practice as Sophomores We were told to watch out for these two moves, I pulled one on He has passed away but I will not use his name even though I can). I stood straight up when the ball was snapped, when He stood up looking at Me as to say what the? I ducked down and blocked Him out of the play. He was a little bit pissed to say the least. That was Our senior year. That same year We were playing (another town) and getting beat. They kept running the same play between the Guard and Tackle positions. At halftime the Coach said for the Tackles to slant and fill the gap, We won the game. The next day the JV team went to Their field. Nobody told Me to line up like that I just did as We were told the night before. They hiked the ball and I stopped the running back for a loss on the first play. It was like a blur, I really don't even remember a lot of the game, but I did it on every play. I can't say for certain because I really don't remember a lot about it, but I am quite certain I made every tackle. At halftime the Coaches usually have a lot to say on this and that, but the head Coach didn't say a whole lot. I even had a chance for a touchdown. I don't know how the fumble was caused or remember even chasing the ball. What I do remember was Me and another Player were the only two around the ball. I told Him to pick it up and I'll block, he had fear in His eyes. Before I could jump on it one of the Guys from the other team finally recovered it. I never saw anything in the paper about that game either. Which is odd, every little thing that happened back then was in the paper. We won 7-0. I am curious how many negative yards They had, I am positive They never reached the line of scrimmage once. One thing I can say about Me was that if I got My hands on You You were on the ground, I never missed a tackle. I always stood the Guy up on the other side of the ball as well, that's what You want to do.

I look back now and see I should have wrestled more, I went out for one season. If I remember right I only had three or four losses. Dad used to wrestle Me until I had the one season, I beat Him pretty quick and He quit trying Me. I wasn't all that great at it, but JV You're not wrestling the Studs so it wasn't all that bad.

I started working at a school in town as an after

school janitor, that is where I met a real Jerk, Jerk #1. I look back and see right through Him and His Pal another real Jerk, Jerk #2. They needed a ride to the senior keg out at the lake so I was asked if I wanted to go. I had a car. Once there I never saw Them the rest of the night.

Other than still being yelled at by My Sister, and being bullied on the football team, life went on. I even started dating My senior year. It was a blind date and She found Someone else instead. Then I dated Her Friend a few times, but that didn't last too long either. After the senior football season was over I did find a steady Girl. Jerk #1 was dating Her sister and the Girls lived ten miles out of town, again He needed a ride again I see now. The drinking age was nineteen in (a cold state) then and I had to shave already, so it was nothing to go to (cannot say it) liquors and buy a couple bottles of wine and go parking. I was pretty slow, but She didn't mind. Dad never took Me aside and gave Me any advice, just let the Boy figure it out Himself. Bad parenting for certain. I do have to add something in here. I had a Kid from school tell me that some Kid was about to hit My Girl one day. The first real Jerk was riding with Me when the same Kid was crossing the street on His bike one afternoon when I was driving down the road. I never even came close to running Him over, I just hit the gas pedal. I even ran into that same Kid twenty years later and apologized to him and explained My actions. I really doubt it now if He was going to hit Her, People were just trying to get the slow Kid into a fight again. My Girl and I lasted the rest of the school year though and then Her Family moved to (another state). I worked all summer long on road construction and then lit out heading south. I have to say I wasn't the Boy I was in high school anymore, while working in (another town in a cold place) I chased any Girl that looked My way. I hadn't learned to be faithful yet.

It was in (that other town) that People found out how dangerous I really am. I was working for a Friend's Dad and one day at lunch this Friend told Me to "Move Your feet!". When I just looked at Him He said "I told You to move Your feet!" and grabbed them and flipped Me out of My chair. It was a reflex to jump up and put Him in a headlock. It ended like many of My squabbles in life always did, I asked Him if He was through and then let him up. I really never liked that Jerk much to begin with to be honest.

This starts another whole chapter of My life.

THE KID TURNED WILD

When I made it to (somewhere where I moved) I couldn't find work, I soon talked My Girl into running away with Me to (another state). We stayed at My Aunt and Uncle's for a few months and then went back to (that cold place).

While in (oops, can't say it) the only jobs I could find were temporary factory jobs through a temp worker place, not enough to really support Ourselves on. As soon as We were in (the cold place) I got My first real Carpenter job, it was for a modular home builder (another I am not allowed to say). Half of the People My age worked there at some point.

Me and My Girl never fought really, but soon She decided it was time to go home. I bought Her a plane ticket and She went home on Christmas day.

Soon after I was laid off and wound up working different jobs, (no names allowed) and a floor hand on well service rigs. But after a while I felt I needed to go back to My Girl. We wrote back and forth and I called and talked to Her, until Her dad would hang up on Us. I thought We were still a couple, not even close. She led Me on is all.

When I made it back down there I went right up to her Dad. He told Me that if I hadn't done what I just did He would have whooped My ass for Me. My Girl sure let Me know then We were through. Would have saved Me some grief if I knew before I moved down there.

For the next few months all I did was try to keep food on the table. My first job I found was while walking around looking, it was at a truck stop fixing tires. I had no idea how far I had walked until the next morning going to work, it was a good hike. When I got home that night, I was staying with My Girls Brother and His Wife, Her Brother said the hell with that job and I went to work with Him and the Guy that went with Me who went with Me from (a town in a cold state). We hauled pulpwood all day long. That didn't last all that long and soon We became Hod Tenders for some Masons. Then I wound up as a Carpenter's Helper on a bridge. All of these jobs paid three dollars an hour, We usually had to steal gas to get around.

It was at that time I was introduced to hallucinogens. My Girl's brother and the Guy that went with Me to some state had went out and picked some mushrooms and made tea out of them, Magic Mushrooms they are called. At first I turned them down but after a while I took a big swig of Her Brother's 'shroom tea. When they didn't do anything I took another drink. I was talking to My Girl's brother who was coming down and then walked out of the bedroom. When I walked into the kitchen the dog and cat saw Me and jumped into the air and took off. That sent Me running across the living room and outside. I stopped outside and was leaning against the wall when I looked up and saw the Guy that came with Me looking at Me like what the hell just happened. I looked down and then back up but He was gone, when I went in to see where He went He was rolling on the ground laughing. That started me to laugh and then My Girl's brother came out. When He saw Us He too started laughing. All three of Us laughed for so long I really can't say how long it lasted. Finally as We were laughing at everything that took place the (damn, can't say it) was on the TV. There was an old Man doing a death defying belly flop. I stopped laughing and got serious and told Them what was taking place. We were on the edge of Our seats when He hit the water, when He stood up all three of us jumped to Our feet and cheered. What a wild day that was.

It was right after this My Girl's Brother decided to try to take His 'shroom tea to (a cold state). He didn't do so well. The Guy that came along decided to head out as well and got lost in (a big state) for a while He told Me later. That was when another Friend showed up. I told Him We weren't eating all that well and He went into the kitchen. He said We had all kinds of food. He took some flour, added a little salt and made fry bread. A Native American feast. Add a little ketchup and it was the best meal I had eaten in a while, honestly.

It wasn't long after that I figured it was time to get the hell out of Dodge. My Girl's Brother dropped My other Friend that just came down and Me off on (an interstate). As soon as We were out of the car a couple of religious Gents heading to (a big city) stopped and picked Us up. My Girl's Brother hadn't even turned around yet. They gave Us a sandwich and a fruit pastry and told us to hop in the back of the truck. By that evening We made it all the way to (a city north of the big city). We were standing on the side of the freeway when a Gal in a Cadillac pulled up, My Friend was suspicious because She had already cruised by. I was in the front seat while He jumped in the back. After a while She looked at Me and asked where We were coming from. I told Her and She asked "Ya'll had time to get horny yet?". I said I guess so. She then asked if She could give me head. I looked back at My Friend and asked what do you think. He didn't hear Her. I told Her She would have to tell Him, when She did His jaw dropped. She took Us to a ballpark where You could see a (can't say it). My Friend was paranoid, He was sure We were being set up. Not Me though I let Her have her fun. When I finished I got out and told My Friend it was His turn, He said nope.

As soon as She dropped Us off back at the freeway an old Boy in a (some car) picked Us up and gave Us a ride into (a big state). We sat in one spot all night. My Friend and Me played frisbee in the middle of the Interstate that night, there were no cars. The next day We made it to (a city in the big state) and then out to somewhere on (a highway). That was where two vehicles stopped at once. It turned out They needed some Workers. I ran a cutting torch and We stacked pipe. They fed Us well and gave Us hotel money or cash for the day, whatever We decided. I told My Friend let's keep going and We caught another ride down the road.

When We hit (another state) We had been riding with this Fella since (a big state). Around (somewhere in that other state) My Friend saw an old Tool Pusher He knew on the highway as We passed Him. He held up Our sign saying (a cold place) and the old Boy pulled over. He offered Us both jobs, it turned out to be one of the best jobs I have ever had too.

It was right after My Friend and Me made it back to (a town in that cold place) I showed Everybody around Me that day how stupid I really am. We walked into the (not allowed), Later (can't say it), and there was a Girl taking orders. When Our eyes met She had love in Her eyes. All I saw was this little Kid and looked away, no shit. She comes back into the story a little while later.

We started out working in the yard, putting a motor in a suburban. Then We worked from midnight to noon on top of a mountain seventy miles from the house. It was fifty percent dirt road all the way. An old Hippy, the Driller, was usually late picking Us up so I had to make up time. We caught a lot of air on the way to the Mountain. One thing for sure, We were never late.

I started out running tongs then went to throwing chain, before long I was the derrick hand. Damn We had a lot of fun back then. Making pretty good money for a nineteen year old Kid. That's when My Family set Me up again. I went and took out a $900 loan to put a brand new motor in My pickup. It had been sitting for quite a spell by then. My sister said She needed to borrow $500. Then She said She wasn't going to pay it back. Later She told Me Mom told Her to do it. What a rotten thing to do. That truck was a 1971 short box special edition, You can not find that exact style now I have looked. It was such a rare truck My Girl's Dad wanted to trade Me straight across for a 1967 (baddass) Car. I told Him I didn't have a clear title on it or I would have. It was one of those things I never thought about after that. I made enough money that I could have fixed it up, but that was when the Boy really began to party.

Back then I smoked so much pot it looks ridiculous to Me now. That and hanging out at the Bar down stairs shooting pool. Then there was (a disco) across the street, it was a Disco. Even though We were hippies We went there every Wednesday night for Ladies night. I never slept on Wednesday. Of course We also frequented (a shame it closed), one of the best Bars You'll ever find too. During the day it was a restaurant and at night a Rock and Roll Bar. And there was always Somebody starting a kegger somewhere. We were young and dumb that's a fact.

That was when I first really started to get into Rock and Roll. My album collection was impressive for sure. I was a stoned Kid that drank a lot and listened to Rock music, that sums it up.

It was about this time that Kid that fell in love with Me was hanging out with Her Friends down the hall in the apartment building I lived in. One night I saw Them coming down the street and knew the Fella that was getting Them stoned wasn't at home so I rushed the Boy's with Me up the stairs and timed it just right and Told Them over the intercom to come up to My place. The Boy's with me asked Her and one of Her friends to go to another apartment and listen to Them play the guitar. It wasn't long afterwards that there was a knock on the door, She came back and told her Friend to go upstairs. She knew what She wanted. We sat together on the couch and with a shaking hand I put My hand on Her knee, after that We were a couple. I sure fucked that up though.

I hate Myself now when I say I wasn't even faithful to Her. I tried to ignore a married Gal one night at the Disco, but Her persistence paid off. I don't know if My Sweetheart ever knew, but that was not Our downfall. Being the Children We were all We ever really did was make out. One night, I hate to disrespect Her here but I have to say what took place, I had Her naked and performed oral sex on Her. I know what it looks like when a Gal has an orgasm, it was on Her face that I did something right. When I told Her I wanted to make love She asked what if She got pregnant. I was about to say something when the intercom buzzed. In My innocence I got up to answer it. When I made it to the hall I turned and looked back. What I saw was the most beautiful body I had ever seen before, I stood slack jawed. My words were saved by the bell for some dumb reason. I ran, real fast too, and answered the buzzer. Then I ran at top speed back to My gorgeous young Sweetheart. She was under the covers with them pulled up to her chin and had a terrified look on Her face. I do not claim to be intelligent Folks,

My sorry ass jumped right on top of Her. It wasn't long before She said it was time for Her to go home. She told Me We were through right after that. Pain? I have attempted suicide a few times, that is another story all together.

I was working in the (don't believe I can say where) then. I was a Kid with long hair working on a crew full of Rednecks. Right after My Sweetheart and I went Our own way I was fired for not flagging the ground like I was supposed to do as a prober in the pits. I continually turned in faulty geiger counters except one night, that's all it took. I spent the next three months as a recluse. I was heartbroken really. I went into a state of depression. Being winter in (a cold place) sometimes jobs were tough to find, and I didn't really feel like looking. I finally went back to check on a job I had applied for, They said They had been trying to contact Me. I gave Them My Parents number, but Nobody bothered to tell Me They had called.

It was during this depression stage that a Girl always came around. She was a fifteen year old Kid that the Jerk#1 knew. I should have been rude and told Her to stop hanging out. I never really talked to Her, She just hung out. All I did was sit really, and listen to the stereo. One night a Kid We knew around town brought Her by and asked if They could borrow My bed, Yes I am that slow, I said alright. (another one that died but I will not use his name) was His name, the Jerk left Her there when He was done. The first Jerk came by later and when I told Him She was in My bed He made it in there quick. After He was through He left as well. I sat there for quite a spell before I said what the hell and went in. She accepted Me at first and then said "You're not (no names can be used)" and rolled over. Hell She knew who it was, the light was on in the other room and You could see everything in the bedroom. I was already naked so I went ahead and pushed Myself in Her and then just quit and left the room. She stayed in My bed all night long while I slept on the couch. The next night She came by. I was sitting on the couch and She was hanging Her legs all over Me, I ignored Her. She finally got up to leave and said "Thanks", for not trying anything. I never saw that Kid again after that.

It's needless to say it but all the Boys that I hung around with were Losers. The only Girls the first Jerk and another Kid brought around were fifteen year olds. They tried to set Me up with Them but I didn't want little Girls around. I grew up with a brutal sister, I sure as hell didn't want a Child. My Sweetheart was different though, that damn Kid fell in love with the Boy. I had even spent some time watching football with Her Dad, We weren't hiding anything.

There were a few things that took place then due to My innocence. Like the time I started crying for no reason in front of another Friend. And then the time My landlord came over and said He had just caulked My neighbors shower and that He needed to use Mine. Well the same Kid I broke down and cried in front of happened to come by when My neighbor was getting out of the shower. My hair was wet because I had just finished before My neighbor came by, I got real nervous thinking They would all think We were Gay. I was so boneheaded as a Kid I told that first Jerk that a married Gal He brought by mouth tasted like sperm too, it tasted funny is all. We were all having Our way with Her. She was a Friend's sister in law. That first Jerk was the one that set Me up with her, real Cads We were in all actuality. She is the exception as far as what They brought around, at least She wasn't fifteen. For the record though, I sure as hell do not know how sperm tastes either. Just a dumb Kid that never thought things through before He spoke.

Speaking of, I told the Friend I cried for what His Sister in law was doing. I wrecked a home then for certain. But hell the Girl slept with Everybody around.

Soon after I started working at a lumber yard that spring a strange occurrence took place. I had just got home on a Friday night and taken a shower. There was a knock on the door, when I opened it a Gal I knew named (I could use Her name too, but won't) was there. She asked if I wanted to buy some acid. My very words were, I don't know, I guess so. As soon as I took it I went to put on some music, (a rock group) was on the turntable ready to play. Acid rock. On the very next Friday the exact same thing happened. This time there was a cassette of (another rock group) on top of the stereo. It tells You that You are going to be a Rockstar. On My next payday I went and bought My first guitar. A couple days later My Pal the first Jerk said that Our Friend the second Jerk wanted me to join them in a band. I had no idea on how to play an instrument. This part will come back into this story in a big way later.

After that first acid trip it became more frequent too. The one that really sticks out is when (the second one to die) set Me up with mushroom spores. Right afterwards the second Jerk wound up riding along with Us. His words to Me were "When You think of Someone They think back", He called it Karma. I look back now and see where all of this was leading to altering My mind and life. What comes into the story at the end will really show how this second Jerk character really is. The second Jerk would also look at me and just say (I can't say it. And it really ruins the story to Me), meaning I was a Child to Him.

It was sometime before then that I was set up with a drug deal, through the first Jerk, in which I never received any drugs. I look back now and see how blind I was. The drugs were mushrooms grown in (a hot state), it would be rough to grow them in such an area for certain. I was told when He drove into a parking lot We were hanging out in that I didn't have any balls if I didn't confront Him. I looked at a Friend there who said it and saw what He meant and walked over to this Assholes car. Said Asshole was an ex (a respectable group of Men) and really thought He was hot shit, still does I feel, so I walked over and demanded My money. He just laughed and said "You'll never see that money" that's when I hit Him. It wasn't even near a rough punch either. I walked around to the other side of the car to let Him get out so We could fight. When I turned around He was almost on top of Me. My foot stopped an inch from his face. He stopped dead in His tracks and We stood there like that until He slowly turned and looked at My foot before knocking it down. It wasn't much of a fight I can say, but He sure as hell couldn't touch Me. He even said to stop moving so he could hit Me, I ain't that dumb.

It was right after that that I told Myself it was time to get the hell out of (the town in the cold place). (a city in that big state) sounded like a good place to go.

HELL BENT FOR (A BIG STATE)

I was getting ready to head out for (the city in that big state) when a name popped into My head. You will see it clearly later when I say head games were being played with My life, I feel that is why this Persons name jumped into My head. Well I asked if He wanted to go along and We soon left for (the big state).

The trip was pretty uneventful until We reached (another city in that big state). We were given a ride by some Kids that took Us way off of the freeway and dropped Us off. He broke a bottle like You see in the movies and was going to attack one of Them until I told Him to knock it off. We were lucky enough to have an older Gentleman offer Us a ride back to the freeway.

It took Us three days hitchhiking to make it to (a city in a big state). We stashed Our packs and went exploring the city. We walked from (can't say) all the way to the river downtown, in those days We walked everywhere so it seemed like nothing. When We made it back to Our stash spot I grabbed one pack and handed it to the Kid that went with me then reached for the other. By that time the Fire Ants were already to My elbow. Them little Bastards sure can bite I tell Ya.

The next day We went to a laundromat and cleaned out the ants. When We left and were walking down the street an old Boy pulled up and said We looked like We needed to go to the lake. We wound up at (better not say it), a nude beach. After hanging out, naked of course, Someone said that the news People were there. I was sitting there with some Gal and Her plaything as it sounded by the way She talked when the news Ladies said just act natural. The Guys there started acting all goofy and jumping wildly into the water. After it all calmed down I walked over and casually dived in for Them.

The next day We figured We had better start looking for work. He went one way and I another. When We met up He had found a carpenter job. He didn't tell Me He saw a job across from where We were dropped off, that's where He got hired. When I went and talked to the Boss He said I didn't have enough tools, but if I showed back up with them I would have a job. I went to a lumberyard and stole a cloth tool pouch and then saw a phone company van and opened the back door and grabbed a hardhat. That is what I showed up with and went to work.

I spent the rest of the summer hanging gyp rock on the buildings with a Black Man. He was a one hell of a hand too. Me and Him slept under a bridge under the freeway while construction was going on and then finally just moved right onto the jobsite We were working on. One night We wandered down to (I really want to say this one, but can't). The (a rock group) were playing but We never went inside. About the time We were going to leave We were asked by this Guy if We needed a ride, We wound up bar hopping. Then He took Us back to the job and dropped us off. It's strange how He wanted Me to sleep in the same area as Him that night, We both had a camp set up where We slept. Right there on the job We just set up house. We ran a garden hose in and showered every night. I cut a hole in one of the boxes with mirrors in it for the buildings and used it for shaving. We definitely made Ourselves at home.

On the night We went bar hopping Somebody stole My guitar, I am pretty sure looking back that it was My Pal just being a Prick because I didn't sleep where He wanted Me to. I don't know why I didn't keep My guitar where My camp was for sure.

We didn't make much money, I think We were only making like $3.25 an hour, so We picked up all the pop bottles on the job everyday after work and cashed them in to eat. We usually bought some bread and

I would steal some ham. One day I stole a pound of hamburger and We went to one of the Guys from the crew's apartment to cook it. We spent a lot of time at that apartment with Him and His Girlfriend. He was a wild Kid really. We got to know Him and His Girl real good too. We were always doing something with those two.

After living like We had been for a while We finally rented an apartment across the street from this couple. Back then You could find a two bedroom for $250 a month pretty easily.

Being asked to join a band like I was, I figured I needed a new instrument about that time. The first Jerk said the second Jerk was going to teach Me how to play bass so I went to the music store around the corner and bought a whole bass set up, amp and all. I never really jammed with the amp on, I just practiced with the bass unplugged mainly, but I was catching on.

Sometime around then We were all sitting at a (another I cannot mention) a few miles down the road when a hitchhiker showed up. The Kid that came along was always making new friends and before You knew it He had invited this guy to stay at Our place. He and I hit it off right away too. It was also around this time that Everybody wanted to do acid for some reason. I never once contacted My Friends in (a cold place) but I am sure the Kid that came along kept in close touch with the first Jerk. I never even thought about it at the time but when They finally showed up in (a city in a big state) They knew exactly where We lived.

Right after the acid started popping up the Hitchhiker and Me took some and took off exploring the night. We went to some High School and tried to sneak into a football game. After We found no way in We were leaving when the Gentleman on the PA said something about Us walking out in a field. I was wearing a white shirt and He mentioned it. This took place right about the time I started tripping.

After that We walked over to a strip club. That was an interesting experience in itself. One old Boy pulled out a wad of cash and said He didn't have enough money to buy drugs. Another one, a Black Man, said His name was Farse. When We left there We wound up walking around the (a wealthy) hotel. That is when My life was about to make one of the biggest changes I have seen.

When We reached the top floor of the hotel there was a party going on. When We walked past the doors were open and in one room was a group of Ladies. I told the hitchhiker to ask Them who's buying the drinks. They didn't seem too impressed so We headed on. When We made it back downstairs I told the Hitchhiker let's go back. We each took different elevators, I never saw Him the rest of the night.

When I got back to the party I just walked past and went to the staircase at the end of the hall. There I opened the door and acted like I was leaving but stood there against the wall just listening. One Woman said People like Her won't stay around very long, or something to that effect. I didn't fool Anybody They knew I was there. So I again opened the door and acted like I had come back and walked over to the party. There was a Man standing in the hall and We started talking. Pretty soon He told Me to go on in and get Myself a drink. As soon as I walked in one of the Gals from when the Hitchhiker asked about the drinks came straight over to Me and said "alright then let's go". All I could do was stagger backwards in shock. Then when I got My self control back I turned and walked away from Her.

When I finally made it to the bar and had a Gal there make Me a drink, another young Woman came over and sat down near Me. I was too innocent to understand why. The way She did it I know now was to let Me know She was interested, and She was not going to treat Me the way the other Gal did. Before long I struck up a conversation with another Gal at the party, I even told Her I was doing acid that night. The whole time I was talking to Her I kept looking at this old Gentleman sitting behind Her.. He just kept looking at Me with a huge smile on His face. Then when I was talking to another man that night I told Him about the first Jerk and the second Jerk wanting to start a band. He told Me He had connections, but I told him We were really just starting and nothing was really going yet.

By the end of the night I was flying pretty high and I was talking to another Woman. We were standing by a window and You could see the job We worked on right next door. The Kid lost a bit of His senses right then, I told her that not too long ago I was living on that site, but here I am now. That's when I figured I had better leave. I said My name is (not allowed to print it) and I am from (a town in a cold place). I don't really know what happened here tonight and then something I'm not really sure what it was. That's when one of the Men there got in a Karate stance and asked Me if I wanted to fight. I just laughed and said no and shook His hand and left. I didn't even notice, but by that time of the night most of the People that were there had left, I am pretty sure it was because of me too.

The very next weekend the Kid I worked with and the Fella that came along wanted to trip again, this time they gave Me a half a hit of four way window pane, meaning two full hits really, and a black molly, speed. I have to say this here, I had the same reaction every time I was asked to do acid, I don't know, I guess so was My response. I didn't even question why the

Hitchhiker had left, the fella that came along just told Me He took off. I think the reason was He wanted no part of what They were up to.

After a while, when the acid started to kick in, the Kid I worked with and the Fella that came along came in where I was sitting in My apartment and handed Me a (a very old dirty magazine company's magazine) and then turned and left Me there alone. I didn't see them again until the next day. The front page of this magazine said (this part stays) "Stoned Hippy carries along hallucinogens". I knew right away it was about Me. At that time I had shoulder length hair. At the party I wore a white western shirt and had flip flops on. I also had a big white tooth earring in My ear as well, I was living the part that's for damn sure. I took My time and read every single page in it, even the ads, until I got to the article about the Hippy. I didn't want to read about My dumbass being at that party. At one point though while going through it I did see My name in it near the rear, You know how They always continue a story. After that night I never read another article in it, I just tossed it on the coffee table for all to read.

I was wide awake for two and a half days that weekend, and I have never been the same since. I never even thought about it until years later, neither one of those two Jerks that night did near as much acid as I did. And afterwards They explained to Me that They always just held it in Their mouths for a while and then spit it out to keep from getting the full effects of it.

I believe it was Saturday night when I was sitting there listening to the radio when a neighbor Kid came over. After a while He said "I think They want You to play Your guitar" I looked at Him and said I know what They want, what do You want? He didn't hang around long after that.

Like I say. I haven't been the same after that weekend.

FAIR WEATHER FRIENDS

It was a few months after that night I spent with the (old dirty magazine company's magazine) that the first Jerk and the second Jerk moved to (a city in a big state). It wasn't all that long after that when the Fella that came along disappeared as well.

It was at this time that the first Jerk started acting differently towards Me. He would say stuff just to piss Me off. More than once I made Him stop His car and I got out and walked. Then there was the time the second Jerk was singing a song, He was just making stuff up while We were listening. He sang "I don't like You Babe" and looked straight at Me. I left the room and actually cried over it, yea I'm pretty soft to be honest.

Other than these two acting hard towards Me, life was actually going pretty good for Me then. I wasn't shy at all and quite often got lucky as it's known. The Gal across the street and I had spent some time and every now and again I was able to pick up a Woman here and there. To show You how it was for Me I have to mention a time at (a great place in the city in the big state). Me and the first Jerk were walking around and everytime I went by this one spot this Gal kept staring at Me. And every time there was a different Fella there trying to get to know her. One time We were walking by and I motioned for her to come on, She got a good laugh out of that. When We finally came by and there were no Guys sitting there I made a beeline over to Her. We sat and talked to Her and Her Friend for a while until She said She needed a ride home. The first Jerk was the one with the car so He jumped in and said He'd take Her home. He wasn't gone long, She blew Him off fast. Looking back now I know for a fact I would punch the Son of a Bitch for doing that. I never once saw that piece of crap with a Woman back then. The only Gal He did date was right before Our falling out, She was a Teenager and They went out once. I never once had to have a Chaperone on a date, Her Mom made Them take one along. Sorry piece of shit was still chasing little Girls, He really thought He was something I tell You.

I had been working for the same company since We arrived in (a city in a big state), the first Jerk wound up getting a job there too. He was the one with a car so We all rode to the Bosses house and went from there. One morning He made Me late and I missed

My ride with The Boss so I worked all day with His Son instead. When We made it back to the house that afternoon The Boss gave Me My check and said He didn't need any part timers and fired me. Another Employee We had for a while was working for a construction company and I hired on with Them right away. That went alright for a while until things went sour there too. We were told one day by the Boss that if We needed a cut use the scrap, if it was a full piece grab a new one. This old employee was cutting for Me and another hand when I went over and grabbed a full piece. He started bossing Me around and telling Me We were supposed to use the old stuff. I told him it was a full piece so I was doing as We were told. He got mad and said I was to use the old stuff and then pulled His hammer out as if He was going to attack me with it. I was the one that walked away from fights, but not this time. I started taking off My tool belt and He knew I was pissed. He put His hammer away and picked up His saw and pulled the guard back and was going to use it as a weapon. The Guy working with Me said "I'll unplug it" I put My tools back on and said He wasn't worth it. I went and worked with another crew. A few years later We were at a house of a Gal We knew and that old employee was there. He told the story in His own version, I corrected Him and told it as it happened. When I got to the not worth it part

I was about ready to flip the table over on Him and kick His ass. That old employee looked stout but He always wanted to wrestle with Me before, I handled Him easily everytime.

While I was working on that same job They put Me with two other carpenters. We were hanging siding. I was on one end and one of Them on the other. We had to measure the lap in the siding everytime. We hung a wall one day and on the next day the Boss said I was fired because I had My side all screwed up. I told Him no I was on this side and showed Him with My tape that all of my measurements were the exact same. He looked up and saw a nail I forgot to pull and said something about it then said all three of us were fired. Damn My luck huh.

It took Me a while before I found a job after that. The first Jerk had started selling Black Mollies He was getting from that neighbor Kid that said something while I was listening to the radio while tripping that night and gave Me a hundred lot to sell until I got a job. We were in a bar, (the best bar around then), We went to a lot and I was selling them just to get beer. When I saw a Guy with real long hair I asked Him if He wanted some. He said sure and let's go smoke a joint while We're at it. I told Him I was just selling them until I found work. He and His partner were looking for Someone and I found a job finally. I'll tell You I became pretty damn fast at driving nails, but this Gentleman is still the fastest I have ever seen.

It wasn't too long after that when the first Jerk showed His true colors. I was always picking around on the guitar, I barely knew but a few chords is all at that time. I was sitting there fumbling with it when the jerk told Me I sucked at it. I told Him I was just learning. That's when He screamed at Me "I'm better than You are and You know it!". That ticked me off a little and I told Him it was His (some state) ignorance showing. That hit the right nerve and he did what others have done, made a mistake, He charged Me. I was standing there with His guitar in My hands when He started towards me, I busted it over His head. Gashed His skull real nicely too. I was in shock and it was all over my face, I stood there and looked at Him in disbelief. He tackled me and drew back His fist. His blood was filling My eyes and I couldn't keep them open so I grabbed His arm and clamped His other one to where he couldn't use it either. As I did with the Kid in (a town in the cold place) I asked Him if He was through and let Him get up.

He jumped in His car and took off. When He made it back He started talking like a real Jerk again. The neighbor Kid and another neighbor were there this time. He told Me "How could I be in a band with a Guy that doesn't have Women?", Hell Jerk, You Sir are an Ignoramus. For one thing You never took a single Woman home the whole time We lived together, fact.

I felt so bad I went across the street and stayed at the Gal across the streets apartment. She was dating a Guy but he wasn't home so I had sex with her that night. He wasn't real happy when He got home later and I was sleeping on the couch.

The next morning I went over to the apartment and packed what I could fit in My backpack and then took My bass and amp to the music store and traded them for an (can't say it either) guitar. Then I started out for (a far away state) with I believe $.36 in My pocket. I looked at that old dirty magazine company's magazine when I was packing and just tossed it on the floor and left it too. It was My apartment, I should have tossed the Bum out really.

A HIGHWAYMAN

In My life I have done a lot of hitchhiking. There is no doubt that I have covered well over 20,000 miles on the road. It used to be fun, but now I don't really feel like dragging My crap across the country on My back anymore.

I'm not really sure how long it took Me to get all the way to (that far away state), but I have some memories from that trip I won't soon forget. I was sitting in (somewhere along the way) when I got a ride from a Fella. When I said I had some carpenter experience He said he could get Me a job and I could stay with him. After I turned Him down he asked "Can I give you head then?". I said no I prefer Women. When He dropped Me off He said He'd be back in half an hour to see if I changed My mind. I grabbed My pack out of the back of His truck and told Him if He came back I'd kill Him. He hauled ass. I could see the fear on His face too. When I walked over to the off ramp I read on the light post where another Hitchhiker wrote He was dropped off there by a Queer. Below it it said, in Spanish Queer is Joto.

My next ride took Me all the way to (a city in a hot state). There I was picked up by a Trucker after walking all night. A Cop went by on the other side of the freeway and told me over the PA that if I was there when he came back I was going to jail. The sign there said it was eighteen miles to the road I walked to, My calves were sore for a few days after that walk. That Trucker dropped me off about two miles from My Aunt and Uncle's house in (somewhere).

It was the same as before, the only work I could find was through (a temp company). I received My tax return and bought a car so I was able to get around some. But I couldn't find a real job for nothing. I did do some carpenter work for Their neighbor and My sister was out there working as a cake decorator and Her Boss had me do some work. That was about it.

Then My ignorance showed up again. We were watching TV and a Friend of my Cousins was lying in front of Me. She was fourteen and was starting to fill out. When I saw Her curves I bent over and kissed Her on the hip. Talk about being shocked, I leaped to My feet and asked her to forgive Me and left the room quickly. My cousin was the only other one in the room at the time, I am sure She told Her Parents because I was confronted about it. Hell, I was just as shocked as Anyone about it.

It wasn't long after that when I headed back to (the big state), (a big town) this time. I sold the junker of a car I had and headed out. My sister had moved to (a big town) and I wound up staying with Her and Her Boyfriend for a while. I found a framing job there pretty quick at least. But I didn't stay in (a big town) all that long and soon hitchhiked back to (a cold state).

When I got to (a town in a cold place) Everybody was telling Me I won't be able to find any work around town, I had a job within a week. It was My first concrete job too. I worked all summer long for that company and wound up buying a pickup off one of the hands there. My dumbass thought I could celebrate and get drunk since I was doing better. I wound up rolling it and nearly killing Myself in the process. Work had slowed down and I had a few hundred saved so back to (a city in a big state) I went.

When I made it to (another city in the big state) I bought a car for $200 and went looking for work. I was hired on within a day or two with a carpenter I wound up staying with for around five years. At first I slept in the car and showered at the Gal that lived across the street before I hit the first Jerk place every night. I gave Her a few bucks every week and ate dinner there too. That was when I met a Cartoonist. He was dealing pot and I bought some off of him a few times. He showed me His (cannot mention such things) cartoon once and said he already had a contract with (not allowed to say it). He acted the part too. He bought a Doberman and made it sit right next to Him everywhere he went. You were not allowed to pet the dog either. He was always saying he couldn't understand Me then. Ya wanta guess My nickname now? (have to omit). You better believe I get called that a lot too. Fuck You Fella. What I always say is that (omitted again) is the coolest one out of the bunch though.

About that time the Guys on the crew said They had a spare mattress at Their place and I could move in. I wound up being the only one of the four that lived there after a while. Sometimes I am disgusted with My ignorance. When I was living there the Owner told me one day He would sell Me the place for $10,000 and he would finance the deal. I told him I didn't think My credit was good enough and declined the offer. There is a small shopping center there now. I am pretty sure it sold for a hell of a lot more than $10,000 after a while. Dumb? Yea, I can say so.

After living on (damn can't say it) Road for a while another (someone from the cold place) showed up in (the city in the big state). Another Pal of the second jerks. I let Him move in and then two more showed up. A third Jerk and a crazy Person and a His low life brother all moved into My little house. All of a sudden I was around People that wanted to do acid again. I was too naive to say no. The second Jerk even hung around a little bit back then. At one point He got the bright idea He could make a living out of going to (another part of the big state)and picking mushrooms and then drying them out and selling them. He came by once and gave Me two ounces. He said it was for rent, He didn't really stay there though. While working for We'll call Him Fred as I had been for a while now it wasn't rare that We would be out of work for a week or two. When the second Jerk gave Me those 'shrooms I just happened to wind up with two weeks off. I tripped everyday. I can say without a doubt it didn't do Me any good at all.

When I worked for Fred I wound up becoming his Foreman. At twenty two I was the Boss. I didn't have a clue what I was doing I discovered quickly enough. The first time I went to hang braces I found out right away that I had a lot to learn. I was his Foreman for three years after that though.

Once a year I would tell Fred I was going to go to (a cold place) and take some time off. I usually had around nine hundred saved and I would send it to Myself in (a cold place). That way if I got robbed on the road They wouldn't get My money. I would take just enough to survive on and hitchhiked to (the town in a cold place). It usually took a week. I had a car some of the times, but I thought it was fun to just be on the road. That is where I really learned to play the guitar too. You get a lot of rides when You're sitting there jamming, that's for sure. After I spent a couple weeks in (a cold place), mainly just partying, I would call Fred and tell Him to send My last paycheck to Me cause I would be broke by then and start back to (the city in the big state). I could go on and on about the experiences I had on those trips too.

It was just after one of those trips, this one was just before I was made Fred's Foreman, when My life was totally destroyed. As I am writing this I am near tears right now just thinking about it. I devastated My life worse than You can imagine. Traumatized is what it is known as really.

LOVE STINKS

I hitchhiked home in the summer of 1982. All kinds of funny things happened on that visit. Like when My sister took Me into town and dropped Me off at the park where the first Jerk was. He got Me stoned and right after My sister came back. We were going to have Our pictures taken. While We were getting photographed the Photographer would say He had to reload or something to that effect. Being a carpenter I was admiring the woodwork in the building and looking around. All four of My sisters sat there and smiled without Me seeing what was taking place as I looked around, He kept filming the whole time. Mom showed Me the pictures later where I looked like I couldn't keep still while We were getting the photos taken, all the Girls had big smiles on Their faces. Yes My Family is an odd one. And I have to say that with so much garbage as They have pulled on Me over the years I really am surprised I even associate with Them, sad I know.

It was right after I made it back to (the city in the

big state) that My fate in life happened. I was in all honesty not much of a Kid. I wasn't faithful to My first Girl or My Sweetheart either one. And I had a bad habit of breaking a few hearts. I hurt a couple Gals because I saw They weren't the one. There was one, She really loved Me but I broke it off. I got slapped for that one too. But in all I don't think I deserved the horrible life I have lived, what happened next tears Me apart inside.

It would have been forty years ago almost to the day. I was in (a cold place) in August then. It would have been around the middle of September when I walked over to a Dancehall on (some) Road, the (well I can't say it) Nightclub. I went almost every Wednesday night because it was Ladies night and the beer was dirt cheap. As I walked around the dancefloor, it was huge too, I came around the corner and saw a very beautiful Woman sitting there all alone. Now this place was packed as always and You had to walk through a huge crowd, but when I saw Her there actually was Nobody even near Her. I told Myself I didn't have a chance but said what the hell and asked Her to dance. My first words to Her once on the dance floor were I moved here to (a big state) because I heard there were a lot of pretty Women, and They were right. If looks could kill I would have been buried that night. That pissed Her off. I told Myself this is going to be tough. I didn't stop there though, I asked Her Her name and told Her Mine and that I was from (a cold state). She told Me She still lived at home and didn't work, that was about the extent of Our conversation. This young Woman, Sweetheart I do not want to sound degrading to You here but I must explain something about You here. This Woman has a very gorgeous body to say the least. Very voluptuous breasts, My dumbass decided to take a look at Her body. I stood there with My eyes bulging and felt like a small Child, the exact feeling I had when I looked at My Sweethearts body. I looked at Her from the neck to Her knees and back up again. When I looked back into Her eyes this Gal had love in Her eyes. All I could do was look into Her eyes. We just continued dancing and looking at each other for the longest time, then Her eyes went from love to pain. Believe Me this is a horrible thing to write down here, it tears My heart out. This poor Gal was in so much pain. Finally Her look of pain turned into one that I knew what She was saying to Me, along with Her gestures and the question in Her eyes She was asking Me why I couldn't do anything. I was in a state of shock really. All I could see was that I did not belong with this beautiful young Woman. The thing that made My mind up for Me was I told Myself I had lost everything good in My life and I would lose Her too. When the song was over I did the only thing I could do, I told Her thanks for the dance and turned away.

When I turned there was a huge crowd of Men standing behind Me, when I reached Them They parted and let Me pass. I came to My senses about that time and made My way to where She had been when I first saw Her. She was gone needless to say.

After that it didn't really sink in for about three months then it hit Me hard. I am a stupid, very stupid Person and that is all I can say about it. It was the same with My Sweetheart, except that took Me two years to understand what happened to Us. It was actually just before I met this Woman that it hit Me what I did to My Sweetheart.

The woman's name is (no names allowed I am told) and (My true love) My God I am in love with You. People, I really hate this life. The pain becomes unbearable sometimes. I'll go into detail later on how excruciating it is.

Within no time after I broke My true loves heart I was dating another Gal, I wound up hurting Her because She wasn't the one for Me. Yes I was a Cad as a Child. I was never taught the proper way to treat Women really. Then just before it all hit Me what happened that night on the dance floor I was dating another Woman, She told Me right up front it was all for fun. I know a Gentleman isn't supposed to tell but I had a lot of sex with both of those girls. After a while the one that was "Just for fun" told Me We had to cool it a bit. It was right after that when what I did to My true love hit Me hard.

For years afterwards if I saw a Woman I told Myself that's not My true love and I wouldn't even try. It took Me a very long time to quit telling Myself that too. What that did to Me was send Me into a depression I have lived with for forty years now. Another thing She did to Me was make Me better Myself in some ways. I didn't even have a car when We met, I bought one real soon though. I was a carefree Kid then, I have changed some over the years but I have to admit I am still quite carefree. The things that happened to Me really make Me the one that doesn't even care. "To the point where You just don't give a damn" and "That's the trouble with Kids now days, They just don't give a damn" are a couple of those sayings I learned that time in '63. Now I did make love some, but it was seldom and nothing meaningful, I turned into a very lonely life after that.

What is disturbing to Me now is that I went back to that place every week for a long time, I had it in My mind that I would see her again, honestly. I know without a doubt there were People there everytime that saw Us do what We did and witnessed this lost Boy looking for His true love. Gad Damn this hurts Me to write this.

THE TOWN DRUNK

For the past four decades I have been what You would call a waste of life. Following (My true love) I turned into a real Drunkard. I was so intent on finding Her I went out every night looking for Her. In My twenties as I was then I could drink a case of beer daily and wouldn't be really smashed drunk either. I would pick up a six pack after work and have that downed before I even went out on the town. I was out until at least two in the morning for two years solid doing that. The way I say it now when I speak of the party life I lived then is that I went to bed early one night and it ruined Me. I found out sleep was good for You.

I mentioned how a Gentleman was the fastest nail driver I had ever seen in My life, Fred was no slouch either. It was rare that We worked side by side then, He would be off doing layout and I ran the framing crew. When We did wind up working together I would get Him into a race. I would stop and put My rig ax, a framing hatchet, away and count out twenty nails. He always got a grin when He saw Me do this. I would look at Him and say I got My twenty. He would stop and count out twenty nails too. We would put Our ax head next to a nail and count off the start, every damn time He would drive His last nail a split second before I sunk Mine. Fred has a 1st and a 2nd place trophy from competition, the 1st place one is taller than Me. We were harder workers than most of You could comprehend. Me and Fred packed a whole bundle of 2x4 studs in a half hour one morning by Ourselves. This is around two hundred and fifty if I remember right. We were running at full speed too. We used to have packing contests quite often to see who could carry more. We never used nail guns until the (not allowed) brand came around. That gun is amazingly fast, You will shoot Yourself if You don't know what You're doing. To this day I have yet to see another carpenter like Fred, I learned a lot from Him.

We had a lot of fun back then as a crew. We would do some crazy shit. Like sectioning off a room in a house or apartment We were working on and play kick block. It's like soccer but a whole lot of pushing and shoving was involved. Back then We hoped it would rain, off to the pool hall or a titty bar it was. I was always giving Him crap saying We needed to go to the lake, one day He said alright and We piled into one of the Guys (nice car I can't say the brand).

After swimming We went to lunch and then We all fell asleep in the garage on the house We were building. When We woke up We rolled up Our tools and went home. One day Fred paid Us at eleven in the morning and We all went to a strip club. At eleven that night They tossed Me out I was so drunk. I wound up tipping one gal $100 that night. Brings a smile to My face seeing Us back then.

For three years I lived like that. In 1995 I quit Fred and after a while finally went out on My own. I didn't do real bad but wasn't very successful at it. At the time I was living in My car, and had to drive from South (of the city in the big state) to North (of the city in the big state) everyday in order to keep a crew. I don't know how We made it either. Everyday We had enough for gas, a joint, a loaf of bread and a (name brand can't say it) each. We would go to (a grocery store) and buy a loaf of bread and I would steal enough meat to feed Us. Then We would go to (not mentioning brand names) and get Our drinks. The first in line would fill His cup and then get back in line and drink His drink and then get another. The whole time We would be filling Our pockets with mustard, mayo or whatever We wanted on Our sandwich. Tough way to live for sure.

After I got My fill of trying to make it like that I wound up giving My car back to a good guy. The Boys all showed up one day a while before that, right before the first Jerk and some Kid named (not allowed). The first Jerk didn't stick around long but (not allowed) did. He was always a Jerk to Me like He was wanting to fight Me. I think it may be the reason the (another one not allowed) showed up. The oldest had a bit more sense than the others and He might have wanted to keep Me from real harm.

I went out of My way to make sure They had a place to live, even went out and bought $100 worth of groceries, in 1985 that was a lot. But after a while I was left with the apartment alone. I never put two and two together that They might have enough money to get Their own place, I was just happy to help. Gullible.

It was right after I was running My own crew I finally gave the car I was buying from a good Guy back to Him and hit the road back to (the cold place).

WHAT NEXT

The first thing I found when I made it back to (a town in the cold place) was a concrete job on the water treatment plant. That lasted until it became too cold to pour concrete. That winter was like before, odd jobs here and there. In the spring I found a job as a cook for a Dude Ranch above (another town in the cold place). I had two years of schooling on cooking in Our trade school during high school. Before I could even start working (nope can't say it) called and I was given the keys to the front door, I was the first one there every morning. That was back when They had the (some size of) pizzas, I would have a mess of them ready before noon. I wasn't there but for around a week when I got a call from a fencing company. Manual labor is more My style than flipping pizzas. I worked there in high school before I met the first Jerk. Back then the assistant Manager told Us to make the pizzas the way We wanted them to be made. I have asked Folks around My age if They remember a line outside to get in, They do. We would have a two inch thick stack of tickets along with the ones We were already making, very very busy. We did not overload them either, but soon the corporate office made Us weigh the ingredients. That was a Teenager's kind of job. The same Manager would set a pitcher of beer in the cooler for Us and We knew where all the parties were after work.

My first day on the job building fence I was given a quarter raise because of how I worked, better than a stick in the eye aye? I worked all summer long until it again was too cold to do anything. It was at that time I fucked up again, My Sweetheart came back into My life.

My Sweetheart pretty much ran (one of the best bars ever), a seriously hot bar in town. I saw Her there a lot too. One night She was sitting alone in the bar when I asked Her to dance. I talked to Her about what had happened years back, all She said was "It's alright". When I asked Her again to dance She declined. One night in the same bar I walked past Her, She had lust in Her eyes. I had seen it before at Fred and His Buddy's birthday party, that Girl shocked Me though. When My Sweetheart looked at Me like that I just kept walking. When I made it to the restroom where I was heading She said "Get that Asshole out of here!". I turned expecting trouble, but when I did the words FULL GROWN MAN were in plain sight over My head, not a soul attempted to engage with me.

It was just after all work ceased with (the fencing crew) I was at the bar again. This time some Kid was handing My sweetheart a big bouquet of roses. She looked at Me with that loving look again, what did I do? I looked at the Fella giving Her the roses and then walked away. It was exactly the same look I saw before and the exact experience I had with Her. I just went on about My life without even giving it a second thought. About a week later (two brothers I can't mention) showed up in town and I hitched a ride with Them back to (the city in the big state). I am curious why They just happened to show up too. Either I was going to be really beaten and the word was out, or Mom didn't want My Sweetheart for a Daughter in Law. I have no clue. When I made it back to (the city in the big state) I called Fred. He said He may be going to (not gonna say it) in the morning and give Him a call later. We wound up in (will not mention the state). Boy was that an experience.

NOT EVEN CLOSE TO BEING DONE

I rode in the back of a pick up truck most of the way from (the city in the big state) to (a state I won't mention). Fred's regular crew rode in front. When they got in the back to sleep They asked Me how I stayed warm. I gave Them My Army issued sleeping bag, You pulled that over You and it was nothing. Best damn sleeping bag ever made.

The first night in (the city in the state We went to) tells the story on how the next ten months or so went.

This is (My name) right here. I walked into the apartment We were given to stay in from Friends of Fred's. There are two bedrooms and I was the first one to enter the apartment. Me? I tossed My stuff in the corner and sat down on the couch. The next one in was El Mexicano We'll call Him and then some Jerk forgot His last name. They both darted into the bedrooms staking claim. Later that night Fred tells the Jerk to find another spot to sleep. I guess He was the Foreman at the time and went in and followed in Fred's footsteps. He told El Mexicano to get out of the bed He was the Boss, El Mexicano said FU. The Jerk flipped the mattress over and the fight was on. That's where I come in.

I went into Fred's room and said You have trouble going on, He said go break it up. So I did so. The kid whose last name I forget didn't like that much. It wasn't long before He was in My face as well. When I finally did get pissed off enough El Mexicano messed it up for Me. The Jerk was getting in My face when I screamed You Mother Fucker and snap kicked towards His face, El Mexicano grabbed Him at that exact moment and threw Him down to continue the fight. My foot went just past the Kid's face whose last name I forgot. When I jerked Him off of El Mexicano and threw Him against the wall My fist was drawn way back ready to strike, that was when Fred came in and stopped it.

I learned from that time in My life that working with the same People, partying with Them, and just seeing Them everyday, You grow to hate each other. Especially when some of those People pick shit all the time.

(the Kid I forgot His last name) quit and went back to (a big state) after a while. That was when We had a twenty man crew. The third Jerk showed up about that time and Jerk #3, El Mexicano and I shared Foremanship. We each had Our sections of the building to control. The Boys We ran were mainly fresh out of school and didn't like being told to carry more than four or five studs. Most Carpenters expect no less than eight studs per arm load as a rule. One Friday Fred gave half of the crew Their checks and said goodbye, the rest hit another gear.

It was a short time after that when (the Kid I can't remember His last name) came back around, I was a Boss this time around. *I was always telling the Boys to drive Their nails straight, it holds the lumber properly. Hell I was told around 1981 to do so by a Framer, Framin' (somebody). The Jerk came back and wasn't nailing properly so I told Him, He didn't care for that. I walked away from the confrontation until I looked over and Jerk #3 was talking to Him. I told Jon to butt out, I taught Jerk #3, and then the kid whose last name eludes me spat some crap about this and that. I walked over to the wall that He had just finished framing and ripped every stud out of the wall very easily, way too easily to be honest. I looked at Him and said You call that framing? Like I said this Boy and Me go back, I have other stories about the Kid whos last name I still can't recall too but I won't elaborate. When I confronted Him in that manner after ripping His wall apart He laughed, another mistake with Me. I hit Him with an open palm in the jaw.*

Like an Ass the still don't remember His last name Kid pulls out His Rig Ax, the framing hatchets We swung daily. I, without thought, grabbed Mine in response. I didn't even try to hit the Boy, I just swung it past His hand saying look out Boy. That did give Him reason to strike I see now. Then I put My ax away and dropped My bags. The next thing I remember is slowing down enough for the Jerk to get away from Me. The next memory? I reached around a tree and took His ax away from Him. My first thoughts were to chase Him but when I turned to do so He was so far away from Me I knew better than to continue. He was running for His life. I do have a scar on the back of My head where He hit Me, all I can guess is I blocked Him when He swung. I can say I would have beat that Kid to death and He knew it too.

I quit that day.

To the Big Boss, You mentioned that day the last time I saw You. Sir, You are a true Gentleman I know from experience. I know You well Sir. I got the shit end of the stick I told You when You mentioned that fight. Sir, I did not chase Him with My ax as You stated, I threw His ax into the abyss Sir.

After I quit I started working for another Framer on the site. His Boys were top hands but the crew was slow to Us. He was trying His damndest to figure out Our system, I taught Him right away. I told Him to buy nail guns, "Do You think They'll help?". All I could do was sympathize with how He couldn't understand the difference.

We wound up going to somewhere proving grounds west of some city for the same company We worked for in (the state I can't mention). I had known Him and His Brothers since the early eighties too. I didn't really get along with the crew. In all honesty it was about that time that crews had a hard time with Me. I usually came in and was made the Boss quick, plus I lived alone. It is a given when a Guy is alone He is shunned. If only They knew My history.

I wound up telling (no names) to take His job and do what He likes with it after a while and found Myself in (a new city) to be exact. That was a wide open area in 1987. There was a bar on ? Street, the (a bar), that had a $10 cover charge. It was all the beer You could drink for ten bucks. You better believe I was there both Friday and Saturday night for certain. They say it's only 3.2 beer but if You drink enough it doesn't matter. I know what I am admitting to here is being a drunk driver, it gets worse. You will be glad to know that now if I want to drink and go out I walk.

I found a job quickly in (not allowed). I have learned to drive around without sunglasses on and look for a certain yellow color, You either see plywood or 2x material that way. I have found more than one job that way. I worked for that company until My cousin I was staying with, the same one that was throwing rocks in the ditch too, told Me He needed room in His house. Nice way to say get lost I know. I got along with Him and His Friends but to be completely honest, the life I have lived has made Me an Outcast to many, I know.

I forgot to mention that while in (the state I am not going to mention, still) I wound up buying a brand new pickup, the only new one ever for Me too. It's a great story on how I picked it up. El Mexicano that I was working with had been saving His money and saw an ad for trucks in the paper. I went along for the ride when He went to look into it. After He was approved the Salesman looked at Me and asked what I had to put down. I told Him I had around two hundred to My name. He left and came back and said if I could come up with two fifty I could get a truck if I ran My name as never having credit before. I looked at El Mexicano and said loan Me fifty. The next day We showed up on the jobsite with two new trucks. When I told My story there were at least three more new ones the next day for the same down payment.

After I left (the new city) I went to (a city in a hot state). It was easy to find work there and I stayed at My cousin's house for a while. She soon told Me I should have found My own place by now and that I had to move, I wound up staying with My sister and

Her Family for a few weeks. I could never save money because I was too wild is the truth.

It was while sleeping on My sisters couch I was driving home from a bar when I was pulled over for speeding, DUI #2. I was released and left town before My court date. (that city in the big state) called My name and off I went.

Once I made it back to (a big state) I found a job with a Friend. We built one hell of a house on (a great lake).

I had contacted Fred about work, He would always hire Me back, and He was setting to head out to (somehwere else) in a short time. I kept working up until We left, just saving cash for the trip. I let My truck payment lapse because of it. When We were in Indy I wound up losing My truck to the repo Man.

We were actually in (a nice place) west of (somewhere else). We were building a large retirement home. Fred made Me the Superintendent over the Framers, My first job as a Super.

We were there during the (a race). The night before the race is knutts to say the least, but the whole month leading up to the race is insane. The infield is packed with People everyday, one hell of a big party for damn sure. There were Men driving around with plexiglass around the driver's seat of Their car. They would pack out a few car loads of beer cans daily for the whole month. I partied all night before the race and said heck with the race the next day and didn't go, My loss I know. I wish I would have gone now.

Fred even had Me sub contract a few jobs plus be the Super on the job, that cost Me. I put the layout mark on the wrong side and built it too big. After that I was screwed.

The night before I found out I wasn't the big Boss anymore something happened at the motel We were staying at. I was asleep when a crew member started beating on My door. The owners daughter and Him had become Lovers, She was the manager of the motel. He was beating on the door yelling She's being raped. When I opened the door He was buck naked and running back towards the office, I took off after Him. When I entered the office there the owner's daughter stood naked. She said He went out the back, there I went after Him. When I ran around the corner another employee was there asking what was happening. He had been working on His car and after I told Him He handed Me a screwdriver and He held the wrench He had and We went to find this Fella. We didn't go far when We ran into an old Friend of Mine that worked with Us, He came walking in from the trees. That old Friend said He took off after Him but He was too fast for Him. I said there's only one road back there let's go and We started back to where He had run.

When We were walking down the road to where He had run a car pulled out. When He saw Us He shut off His lights and hit the gas. That old Friend and the Kid with the tools both jumped out of the way. Me? I stood in the middle of the road as He was gaining speed. When He was about fifteen feet away from Me I leaped to the side and threw the screwdriver I had at His head. If the window would have been rolled down I would have tagged Him in the head. As it was that screwdriver bounced off His window and missed Me by about a foot.

We hauled ass to the motel and jumped in the truck I was driving at the time and tried to catch Him. We were going down a road and saw a similar car and stopped to check it out. While We were looking at it a Cop pulled up, the Gals at the motel had already called the Cops like We told Them to and gave Them a description of the car type. This Officer was watching the car already. None of Us had ID, and He told Us to put Our hands on the hood. I took a step towards Him trying to explain, wrong move, He had His hand on His gun and repeated His order. I won't do that again.

The next day I found out in a rude way I was no longer the Boss. Fred had a Partner that turned out to be a shady Character and He wanted Me out of the position. Fred said just go to (somewhere I had never been before)and I was on the road.

I didn't last very long in (the place I had never been before). I blew a head gasket on My way down and wound up getting ripped off by the Mechanic that I dropped it off with. I soon said Hell I haven't been to (a cold place) for around three years and headed home.

One memory I have from when My truck broke down is that I hitchhiked from the Mechanics shop to (the place I had never been before). I was picked up by an old Boy. He offered Me a beer and a shot of whiskey, both of which were nasty. I drank one each. He was driving like a Wildman and asked Me, "You scared yet?". I said Hell no, Ya oughta see Me drive.

I left (the place I had never been before) hitchhiking but soon said to hell with that and got on a bus. On a layover in (a big city) I had a Black Dude try to sell Me some drugs. After he proved to be crooked and I confronted him He threatened Me with a .22 He said He had. I held Myself in check because I almost slammed His head against the ground. I am dangerous when I strike without thinking, if I have to think about it I don't attack very often. After that the trip was unworthy of writing about.

Once I made it to (the town in the cold place) it went as usual. There was an ad in the paper that said They needed a hard worker, so I went to work soon. The first day on the job, it was for a homeowner, I shoveled top soil for eight hours straight. Other than that I built a sidewalk from moss covered rock that We went to a

Mountain and picked up. Built His chain link fence and did some framing as well. Also I had My first experience with a sprinkler system. There was some time in that era that I even worked on a local farm. These Boys do not pay well I found out. I worked a good forty hours, when the check came through it was for around $125, farm wages aye?

After that I wound up going to (another town in the cold place) on an invite from the Kid from (the town years back where I worked with the Jerk I didn't like) years back. I found work but not enough to make a big impression. I did work for a Gentleman there that taught Me a lot, (can't say His name) was a great Carpenter. I teach Apprentice's to learn from Anybody, two weeks experience and You learned one trick from a Carpenter is valuable in Our trade.

Money was tight so I learned to fish or kill Animals when able just to eat. It has been the story of My life, food availability.

But as always I had to move on. The Kid from (the town where He flipped me) left a note saying I left a dirty knife in the sink, crap! Well My next stop would be (Somewhere). I did leave a gentlemanly note in response. That night I found an airport hanger to sleep in while waiting for My flight. I had enough money to fly for My first time back to (the town in a cold place) at least.

ANOTHER START

When I made it to (somewhere) It was the coldest spot in America at that time -30 with no wind. Living in (a cold state) I know about the cold. In the winter of '78-'79 the high was -30 for a month straight. It would be -45 and warm up to thirty below. In (somewhere) I was staying with My cousins brother-in-law in a small trailer, He had no heat. That army issued sleeping bag sure came in handy. You jumped out of bed and got dressed quick I tell Ya.

The job I found was in a grocery store. It was a small one. The owner told Me He would teach Me to be a meat cutter. Really all I did was mop floors and make sandwiches daily. One day He jumped My ass about changing the water in My mop bucket too much, there was a lot of mud being tracked in and the water would get so dirty it would leave streaks so I changed My water. I told Him here's Your mop then and walked out the door.

The next job I found was setting up trailers. By that

time I was staying at My cousins, it was a good walk to work and at minus thirty Your ears got pretty damn cold by the time You got to a warm spot. All I had was a used pair of snow boots, a sheepskin jacket and long handles on. I had come accustomed to wearing the one piece long johns since working for Jay's fencing, they work better than the two piece type. When setting up trailers You spend a lot of time on the ground crawling underneath the trailers, I never really was so cold I couldn't handle it.

I even made the news while working for Them. We were backing a trailer house into a very tight spot, I was the driver. The owner of the company told Me to do nothing but look directly at Him and nothing else. The Foreman was at the back and with the two communicating backed Me right in. A news crew showed up while We were doing this and filmed the whole thing. The Foreman told me the next day He saw it and I was easy to make out.

On one of Our deliveries We almost flipped a trailer house. I was driving the set up van behind the semi, when We came out of the tunnel west of (somewhere) on (an Interstate) I saw the semi heading down the road by itself. The welds on the hitch broke. The house was heading straight towards a rock wall and My first thought was it was going to be smashed to pieces. We all were surprised when it took a left on its own. Being winter there was snow on the ground. A car had pulled off the road and then back on leaving a rut in the snow. It had hardened enough for the I-beam that had already formed a ski shape to catch it just right and it turned back onto the freeway. I was sure then that it was going to roll but nope it went into the middle of the freeway and stopped. Luck was there for Us for damn sure. To top it off after We had it welded back together and made it back on the road a tire came loose and went shooting out into a field. The Boss jumped My ass over that because I was the one that put the tires on. Neither of Us realized that they were probably loosened due to the near catastrophe We had earlier, the tires held well enough for the damn thing to go all over the road like it did. It wasn't too long after that when I found a job building houses instead.

I found a job building houses for (no names allowed), a mining company there. If You worked for Them Your housing was free. We even had a maid come in weekly. It was a short time and I again was the Foreman.

I had never really gambled a lot until (somewhere). I perfected a system of Blackjack that I see others use in Casinos Today. I sit on third base and watch all the cards. If the dealer needs a card, a six or lower showing, and Everybody in front of You has hit a high card, the next card is a low one on average. And the same goes if They all hit low cards it's a high card coming. I have actually had People tip Me at the table for beating the Dealer.

When I was building those homes I had a fight one night. Me and the Boys I hung out with were sitting at this Gals house. She was saying all sorts of crap about how She likes giving head and taking it doggy style. A couple of the Guys got a bit excited and tried to mess with Her but nothing. Soon We were walking down the street when Her Boyfriend showed up. He took Her down the street and was talking to Her. Pretty soon He was so mad He hit a horse trailer and broke His hand. After that He threw Her down then came walking towards Us. When He got to Us He had a smirk on His face, I backhanded Him. That is when He took off running. I knew I wasn't going to catch Him so I walked to the house They stayed in. He was sitting on the steps when I walked up. As I walked up I moved in stride and kicked Him right in His mouth. I then began to punch His face and head. I didn't even realize that one of the Boys that was with Us before was on the other side of Him beating on Him too. I didn't know His hand was broken and as He was covering up I was punching that hand the whole time. I knew Him for a while and already knew He was one tough Bastard, We just scratched Him really.

After a while of building those houses I wound up

quitting and working for a company hanging sheetrock. We worked for something like two weeks straight to finish the huge ceiling We were hanging. I was so tired when We only had a few sheets left I told the Boss I couldn't go on and went fishing for the rest of the day. When I came back to town I went to the Casino and sat down to play cards. I remember it clearly, I pulled out $10 and lost it pretty fast. I then pulled out $20 and began to win. I put the $30 in one pocket and the $230 I believe it was I had won in another and left. In (somewhere) then there were these little dare devil Punks that rode Their bikes around town. They would shoot out from behind a building and jump right into traffic, I barely missed Them that night. I swerved to miss Them and opened the door and yelled at Them and went on. That's when the red lights came on behind Me. The Cop said He saw Me swerve and open My door but didn't see any Kids. After I was arrested for DUI He said I should have just run over Them instead, I looked at Him and said You already have Me for a DUI what do You want a Manslaughter charge as well. Cops aren't always the nicest People. The reason I was charged for drunk driving is an easy one to see. He told Me to recite the alphabet, too easy I thought to Myself. I said A B C D? A B C D? A B C D? And then looked at Him and asked what comes after D? UI a Buddy of Mine said when I was talking to Him. Yessir DUI #3.

When I went to jail I wasn't all that nice to the Cops, I was a bit pissed off about the whole deal. They tried to slam Me down by jerking My cuffed arms up behind Me. I locked My elbows and all They could do was to pick Me up off the ground. Being a smartass I stepped up on the bench there and asked does that help? Then one of Them grabbed My wrist and I didn't lock it in time, I have had My wrist bent before it hurts. I went limp. They then went through My pockets. I had a small amount of weed on Me and was giving Them shit saying They had a big bust. The next morning I saw some money under the door, My $30 I started with at the Casino. That $200 and some never showed up, nor did I get charged for pot. Marijauna was a felony for that amount in (a state) at the time so I sure as hell didn't mention anything about it.

After I was done with court and all I left the state. I said I hadn't been to (another state) in a while.

BACK HOME

I can say that (another state) is home to Me. I lived there from the age of two until I was thirteen. I am sure if I looked hard enough I could have found a few old classmates still in the area. I did stop in and see the neighbor Kid I kicked before school's Mom though. I used to spend the night there quite a bit. The Kid I kicked before school had a Dad that owned a small grocery store. On Saturday mornings He took Us to the store and We could choose Our own box of cereal, that sure as hell didn't happen at home. His Dad even took the Kid I kicked, Me, and His older Brother to a few (cannot say it) games. One time We had seats just behind the press box, directly behind home plate. A foul ball came straight back towards Us. I had My glove on and went to catch it when some Jerk pushed Me out of the way. His Dad was a pretty heavy set Man and never did anything about it. Knowing My Dad My old Man would have punched Him for it.

When I first made it to (another state)I found a job

in (a town in that state). I worked there as a punch Carpenter and lived in My car. Don't really remember the reason for leaving that company but I found Myself in (not allowed to say where). There I hired on with a concrete company. They were building a parking garage that would have apartments built on top of it. If You were standing at the (can't say where) and looking inland We built the second one on the right.

I found out pretty fast what rent is like in (somewhere) too. I couldn't afford to live there. I did find out that a couple Boys from (a town in a cold state) lived there at the time and looked Them up. I didn't move in or anything but I had a place to crash every now and again.

The places I found to live in were flop houses I guess You'd call them. I rented a room in one that I shared with a couple others, I spent a week or two there is all. One thing that came from that stay is a song. I sat down and said I was going to write a song about My DUI. Playing it for People over the years since I have been asked twice "What are You doing working?". Shoudla is the name of it.

My next rental was a place where I at least had a private room. The bathroom sink was so dirty I refused to shave in it and grew My beard out instead. One night one of the other renters was trying to turn My knob and come in, I had a pistol there but He wasn't serious. I moved again.

Being an experienced Hitchhiker and living in My car a few times I knew how to keep clean. You find a secluded area with a water spigot and You have it made. A Whore bath works in a pinch as well. You go into a gas station restroom and just clean the essentials.

Working for that concrete company I met a few Friends and soon one of the Guys from Work and Me rented a motel room together. That is how a lot of People make it. The house the (a cold state) Boys lived in there were four of Them splitting the rent, that's how You can afford to live in a decent place. I sure as hell couldn't afford anything I could find on My own around then.

Because of My ability to get My ass to work I started moving up a little bit in the company. On one job I was put in charge of the plywood crew. Then I was on two other jobs putting in brackets for the rebar to tie to. That was a learning experience I'd say. The only problem the Big Boss had with Me was I would forget to grab the old plywood for some certain places and use the wrong sheets, I had been decking floors for years by then and it was just a reaction to grab a sheet and go. He let Me know too. As far as the crew liking Me most were cordial, but there were a couple. I can't point fingers, but I had a bolt work loose on the front end of My car and they just don't come loose like that. People are dangerous.

It was when I was at the house of My Friends from (a cold state) I was introduced to crack too. I had never even thought about trying the garbage before. There was a Black Fella that hung around a lot then. We were the only two at the house and He went and got some Cocaine. He taught Me how to make crack and smoke it. That will come into the story later and You will see the problems I had with that junk. Fourteen years or so I have stayed away from that bullshit at least now, straight up garbage is what it is really.

It wasn't very long after Christmas I was laid off, the car I was buying was from another Friend and I gave it back to Him. I knew Him from (a cold state). The car I left (the state before this one) in I had blown the motor not too long after arriving there.

One of the memories from working in (a town) was a pizza place around the corner. On Monday night during MNF it was free beer or pizza I'm not sure. You know where most of the single Guys were on Monday. On one night while We were sitting there one of the Guys was talking to some hard head from (still not allowed to name states) I believe it was. When They got to talking about working in the Union My Friend said He had been a Butcher in the Union. When He said how much He made then the loud mouth said He never made that kind of money as a Butcher. My Friend said You calling Me a Liar? Then turned His back on Him.

This Jerk from wherever started telling Him He boxed golden gloves and wanted to show Him some moves. After telling Him a couple times I stood up and said show Me some moves. He had Me hold My hands up and went to hit them. I blocked everything He threw, they sure didn't look like they were aimed at My hands either. He said I wasn't supposed to move, I told Him that if something is heading towards My face I block it. He sat down and wouldn't look at us. He was a pretty stout looking individual too. That's when I lit into Him. I asked do You know where you are? Drive bys are pretty common right now. All I would have to do is wait for you to get in Your car and follow You and shoot You and it would get blamed on another drive by. He wasn't in the pizza joint long after that. That was in the late '80s and there were quite a few random shootings going on.

(a Friend) was one of the Guys from (a cold state) living in the house. During Christmas We decide to haul ass to (somewhere). While there I was playing Blackjack. I learned something from that night, if Someone is talking to You while You play tell Them to leave You alone. I had a face card and a ten when I looked back the dealer was taking My money, I had Him beat. He flipped over two cards and said I had a fifteen. The Pitboss made Him pay me. I wasn't sober enough to realize I had Him big. I should have asked the time, the table, His ID # and contacted the gaming

commission. Sure I probably never would have made it out of (that place) alive, but I would have tried to get paid.

After being laid off I headed back to (a city in a big state) again. At least this time in (a big state) I stuck it out until the turn of the century.

ANOTHER CHAPTER

I have been across (an interstate) so many times with a pack or a duffle bag thrown over My shoulder it's kind of confusing what happened on this trip or that. On this trip across the (a part of America) I really can't remember anything that really stands out on the trip.

When I made it to (a city in a big state) I worked for Fred for about a week until He found Me a job with a Fella. He lived in (a town in a big state) and I soon found a place to live there. The one thing that stands out from being there was the pronunciation of (a town in a big state), it's (ruins the story not being able to say it) Durnit and Ya better learn it. That was from His youngest.

Some parts of (a big state)? I could go across the street and buy beer, but not on this side of the street. I have been around (another part of the big state) where People were already half drunk and had to drive fifteen miles to get more beer. That My Friends is ridiculous. You are putting Drunks on the road instead of letting Them walk across the street to get more beer, You figure it out.

Anyhow, this fella turned out to be a nice Guy that opened His mouth too much. I had just bought an old Ford truck so I took off back to (a city in a big state). It didn't take long before I had an apartment either.

At that time I was working for a Fella named (can't say it) building track homes in N. (a city). He had an established crew and We kicked some Butt. We actually built a full house, meaning framing the walls and cutting in the roof, in one day. I stayed with Him for quite a while too. The deciding factor for Our departure was when I tripped over a tub wall and fell face first into a wall. I wound up pinching a nerve in My back. To tell You how Carpenters can be, when I told (another Boss) I might have a pinched nerve one of the crew said "You ain't got no pinched nerve". Yes (No name) I did. When You do something and it brings You to Your knees something is wrong Pal.

I received $2,500 from Workmans comp. I went out and found the first really decent ride I had owned since the '87 new one, I bought a 1981 El Camino. I then found a decent place to live. The one I was in wasn't the nicest neighborhood for sure. Sitting in My apartment one day I heard a ping. I told Myself that sounds like a shovel alongside someone's head. I had never heard it before but it definitely was that.

At the time I was living in that apartment building I really screwed up a serious job too. I was hanging sheetrock on the new (some) building on (a road) and was moving up fast. This was for (can't say it), at the time the largest Drywaller in America. From day one the Boss liked Me because I carried a serious hammer. "There's My punch out Man right there" He said on My first day. After that I took on anything thrown My way too. I was lucky to be riding with two Employees that lived in the neighborhood, one said He was quitting and I told (a Pal) the other to put in a word for me. They were the layout crew. I had a lot of layout experience from working with Fred over the years and I knew I could jump right in too. On the first day the Foreman told us to just stand there and not do anything. I guess the Guys had screwed stuff up before. After looking at the plans for a while I said this is elementary layout, all cubicles, so I told the Kid working with Me fuck that let's go. When the Foreman came back He was pissed at first but after rechecking My work I was left alone after that.

My mistake with the company was when a Friend of Mine that I got hired on had a seizure. When the Super asked Me over the radio what happened to a Friend I said that I told Him that I told My Friend He probably got fired. My ass was told next time to keep My fucking mouth shut, right over the company radio. I didn't get a chance to say I also told (another Friend) to go talk to Them about it.

After that My performance went south, I didn't give a shit. I was one of the first laid off. Not too long after that is when I finally received My Workmans comp check and bought the El Camino.

It was around then that My Parents came to (a city in a big state) to visit. When They said They planned on adding on to Their house I said when. I was working for, We'll call Him El Jefe, in South (a big state) when I went to (a cold state) to build the add on. When I came back I went straight back to El Jefe. Boy do I have a memory from S. (a big state). We were working in (somewhere south) when the Boys all wanted to go to (another area) and see the sights. La Zona is where They were headed, Boys town. It is where the Prostitutes hang out. I didn't really have an interest in going but El Jefe said go on and gave Me $100 for the night. Of course I did as the rest and grabbed a Gal and had some fun. When I came out there was a real pretty one there, She wanted nothing to do with Me as far as venturing into the back rooms. I asked Her to dance then and the next thing You know I am stripping down on the dance floor. Somebody came over and said My Friends were about to leave Me and I got dressed and caught up. The Gal I was in the room with earlier gave Me a quaalude and We had been drinking since around noon as well. Hell, I thought I was doing alright.

I worked with El Jefe for quite a while until I told Him

I wasn't going back to (somewhere in that big state) with Them. I started working for another old Friend a Fella I had known for a long time. It was about this time when I started screwing up and smoking crack a lot. It's not like I smoked it everyday, but on the weekends I would go out and get My dumbass messed up pretty good. I worked for this old Friend until He got married and moved to (another apart of the big state). Me and (a Man) who worked with Us went to work for the third Jerk then.

On the night of the old Friend's bachelor party I talked to Fred about doing the trusses on an upcoming job on (really can't say where), He said I had the job. The problem is that when the job came around I wasn't ready to take it on, I was getting too stoned to save any money. I had to let the third Jerk take the job instead. The first day on the job the third Jerk and (a Man) were working together and I was on the forklift. On the way home that night (a Man) said He would wind up killing that SOB if He works with Him much longer, the third Jerk is an arrogant ass. The next day I said to the third Jerk that He should be on the forklift and let Me run the trusses. That Fool made so much money it is sad.

After that job I said to hell with making some Jackass a lot of money and contacted the same old Friend I worked with (a Man) on in (a big city in the big state). He was running jobs for a big company. I showed up with My Nephew and one of the hands from (a town) and started subbing on My own, that was in 1995.

The first year I didn't really make a killing until I did a job prefabbing and hanging arches. They paid I think $35 an arch to build and set. I would build four buildings and turn in two as being complete. Then the next week I would set all four and draw the other two. Each building had something like twenty arches. One week I can't remember what I turned in but My nephew was the only employee I had and after paying Him I had over $2,000 left and decided to go to (not gonna say where) and go play some blackjack. I saw an old Fella in (somewhere) sit at the table and bet $100 on three spots. He was drunker than all hell and walked out with no less than ten grand. I tried it that night in (another town) and was up $3,000 in a few hours. Again when You are winning it seems like Someone always wants to talk to You, I lost that and My two thousand fast.. I left with $300 in My pocket, talk about feeling low.

It wasn't long after that when My Nephew quit Me, I was a hard ass to Him. The Boy was 18 when He showed up with His pants hanging down and His boxers flying for all to see. He moved slower than a snail to boot. That first night He was with Me I told Him You'd better pull Your pants up and get that droop out of Your ass or You won't make it out here. The next day His pants were pulled up and He got His tail in gear. He *is now a Union Representative and the Father of two Boys of His own.*

It was sometime in '96 I did a shearwall holddown job for this big company. His head Man, came over to Me then and told Me if I wanted to take on all of the hardware jobs like the one I was doing I could have them, I soon had eight jobs going at once. After a while I couldn't think of anything but work, I thought it would drive Me insane. I was barely keeping up, I had to nail the imbeds that came out of the concrete before the plywood was on I thought, I know better now. I was getting My work done but couldn't make any money like that. That is when one of the Supers brought a Fella by. He had been in and out of Prison and had some big arms on this Guy. It took a week to teach (My employee) My system and then He did all the inside work and I took care of the outside stuff. After a while I had more money than I knew what to do with.

I still had My weekend crack problem and I liked strip clubs. Also if I had a truck that I didn't really like and it needed some work done I would upgrade and get another one. I averaged $1,500 a week and didn't really work that hard. I didn't pay (My employee) a great wage but He never bought a meal and I always gave Him a little extra each week. If We only worked thirty two hours He still got paid for forty. He told me one day He had never had so much money saved in His life.

His problem was He liked to talk smack, so I finally fired him. A mistake I know, but I found other Guys that could do it. None like Him, He was an animal. I left for a vacation for a week and I still made a $2,500 paycheck that week. There's another story for You, My vacation. It was My Parents anniversary and They were going to renew Their vows. I drove like a Wildman just to make it minutes before the ceremony. My sister informed Me I was giving a speech. As soon as I was out of the shower I was set in front of Family and Friends to open the ball. I had not even a clue what I was supposed to say, but the words came out elegantly. All except the final word. I was going to say welcome to the festivities or something to that effect but My mind went blank. Instead when I got to the word festivities and My mind went blank I just looked at the crowd for a few seconds, and then I said party. They got a good laugh out of it and Nobody gave Me any crap about it either.

For two years I lived like I did in (a big city). On a couple occasions I really went off the deep end spending thousands of dollars on crack, I just gave the garbage away to People around Me. I even had a Fella use My car because He was going to sell it for Me if I bought what They call a cookie I believe it is. That is just a big pile of crack that hasn't been broken up to sell yet. I didn't see Him again and finally turned My car in as stolen. They found it in (somewhere) and I flew out to pick it up.

It was when the Felon was still working for Me that (My true love) really hit Me hard. I literally cried every single day for a solid year. One time it racked me so hard I fell to My knees. I drove to (a city in a big state) and went through the archives of the (newspaper in the city in a big state) and found an ad that was printed just after I hurt Her. "Broken hearted Lady needs Someone to dance His memory away". I posted My own saying, (My true love) where are You? I've come to My senses. The only reply was from a Girl who said She thought it was a Gal She had put advances on. I am a glutton for punishment.

With all the stupid shit I was doing it is amazing I never got caught earlier. I finally did in '97. I just left a strip club and had some cocaine on Me. At first the (a city) Police that pulled Me over for speeding said just go home. Not Me, I called a Dancer I had spent some time with and asked if I could come by. I missed her turn and spun around when (a suburb) Cop pulled me over. That name says it all. He arrested Me for suspicion of DUI and took Me in. When They went through My pockets they found a dollar bill with some coke wrapped up inside of it. The Officer asked "What is this?" I said I didn't have a clue. They kept repeating the question and I kept saying the same thing. Finally I got in front of the Magistrate and He asked Me about it. I told Him I had just left a tittie bar and right before I *left I had just ordered and finished a drink and put the money in My pocket. We locked eyes for a spell and then He crossed out the $5,000 bond on the paper and wrote $3,000. If I do have to lie I can do it, but I don't like to.*

I wound up plea bargaining and doing deferred adjudication, meaning if I did My probation I would not have a felony record. I spent ten months on probation with one dirty UA and then a PI, I spent a full year in (some jail) State Jail. They call them Gladiator Farms.

CONVICT

A Convict is exactly what You get called by the Guards in (a jail). (a jail) is not a maximum security Pen, but it's still the Pen. From the start You hear this rumor that They are going to start good time soon, don't believe it.

The place is a Zoo. They throw You in a dorm with Seventy People in it. Half Black and half White with a few Mexicans tossed in to even it out. I saw at least one fight a week in there. I came close to a few Myself and even grabbed a Kid by the throat that shared bunks with Me. I worked from two in the morning until ten in the kitchen and the Kid was always keeping Me awake. One morning I came in and He's sound asleep, I grabbed My drawer and started opening and closing it and making a hell of a racket. He says what's Your problem? I said how do You like it when You're trying to sleep and some Asshole wakes You up? He said some other crap and I grabbed Him by the throat. He acted like He was going to hit Me so I pinned both His arms down. I told myself I couldn't hit the Boy, He was so weak I had to let Him go. He got up like He was going to do something, after I kicked Him in the chest twice He decided against it. He had Himself moved to another dorm real quick too. I wasn't the only one that was about to kick His ass for Him.

When You go in They make You take some sort of trade class. In the first one I didn't last long because I probably knew more than the Teacher. He sent Me to the Horticultural class after a week in His class. After I finished the class I was set up with a job working in the garden, an Inmate's dream job really. All You can eat vegetables all day long. That went great until I had to take a leak one day. We always stepped behind the classroom and did Our business. One day one of the office People was out for His afternoon walk when I did so. I put Myself back in My pants and never even really peed. When I looked down I saw a dry eraser marker there and picked it up and turned it over to Him. The next thing I know I am called into the Captain's office. He was sitting there and accusing Me of huffing the pen and peeing all over the place. To top it off I had just earned My way out of the crazy dorms. I was in a place where You only had four bunks to a room with a private door. In the others you wore earplugs 24/7 just to keep Your wits about You. The dorm I was put into was way worse than the original one I was in. This one Black Kid in there urged on fights and bet envelopes on the fight. That was when I started working in the kitchen

You learn a lot in a place like that. Like when I went from Dishwasher to Baker I learned how to do yeast hits. We had big vats of dough, if You poke a hole in one end and push all the air from the other end towards You it produces a gas that is similar to a cocaine hit. It only lasts for a few seconds. We had to keep the Guys out of it or We would never have any baked bread.

Another thing I learned are some sayings. One old Boy was told He was going to get His ass kicked, "Is Your kicker broke?", Or "Because We are in Jail does that mean We can be Gay?". Like I said They always said We were going to get good time, meaning You get time off of Your sentence for staying out of trouble, bullshit. I got so tired of it I started My own rumor, it's probably still told there too. I said one day that They were about to start selling blowup dolls on the commissary. I was told that a few months later. Then there are things You learn about like Fifi, or killing You really do not want to explain.

Cigarettes are not allowed in the (a big state) prison system, yet they are there. I was so close to being in a riot over something so simple as a smoke it is scary, The square is where you went to settle Your differences. One day a White Boy and a Black Boy squared off over payment that was never settled between the two. As always You just watch. This time every Black Man in the dorm was in the square. I knew it was about to kick off, the first thing I learned in there was "I won't let 'em beat You down if You won't let 'em beat Me down". My first response was fear. I had a scared feeling come over Me like I had never felt before. My next thoughts were I am three bunks away from the fight, I am going to run across the tops of the bunks and fly into the middle. From there it would be elbows, knees or whatever. Right at that time it dissipated.

I do have a fond memory from (a jail) State Jail though, My name is God Damn. I played a lot of basketball and when I missed I said God Dammit. That became My name. I would be walking along and out of the blue I'd hear Hey God Damn, I liked that part. Other than that, Jail sucks.

I went in on November, 16, 1998. I was released on November, 16, 1999. One full year.

A BRAND NEW CENTURY

Fresh out of (a jail)? When I got out I went to find My vehicle and tools. I made the mistake of trusting another so-called friend. When I went in Dad said He would come to (a big state) and grab My things and keep them safe for me, I said I trust this Guy. When I made it to His house My suburban was gone along with a few other things. I had a 1973 4x4 suburban in which I had just put a rebuilt motor in. It had a Z-71 package and Edelbrock intake and carburetor. The interior was new along with the tires when I bought it, it was a classic. (a Thief) showed Me some half assed paperwork from the city of (some city) saying it was towed for outdated tags and crushed. (a Thief) was so screwed up on Meth and had been fired from the same big company, I can bet money He sold it out from underneath Me.

Being on foot this fella and I found some sub work together that didn't last long. Soon I found some sub work on My own putting in shearwall hardware again. I moved into a (can't mention companies) about two miles down the road and did alright. When the work was finished I wasn't finding much else so I hitchhiked to (a city in a big state). Right away I found a job doing furrdowns and asked Jerk #3 If He'd Partner with Me. On the first morning there He was run off for wearing shorts, He knew better. The construction field has changed a lot since the '80s, no soft soul shoes and no shorts is the rule now. I tried to make a go of it but the Kid I did hire when I told Him how the pay would work He said He couldn't work for Me. That was when I went walking around looking for work and ran into a big company job. I talked Them into having Me build the arches on the job. I didn't even have a saw. All My tools were in storage in (someplace). So I borrowed a saw and cord off of Jerk #3 and went to work the next morning. I built Myself a tent under a tree out of material off the job and lived there while I worked. With just a hammer and a saw I made enough to buy a car the next weekend, a Volkswagen Quantum.

I then ran into an Electrician I knew from (a big city in a big state) who was living in (a town) about thirty miles from the job. He told Me to move in with Him. He owned a house there that He was remodeling. It didn't take long when something happened to My car and it wouldn't start. Before I could get it running I saw a pickup in town and bought it. (Whomever) was the Guy I was living with, He was a good Friend of the Fella that lost my suburban and was a Speed Freak too. He had Me smoking the crap and We worked on His house till all hours of the night.

I really was a mess when smoking either Meth or Crack. I would go into this head trip that I had to explain something, it was so simple to Me. If You understood that I understood what I was saying I would shut up, Nobody ever understood it and I would not be able to quit. It freaked Him out just a bit.

He was giving Me the stuff and what made Me quit and move on was when I was at work I did a line. In My head a voice told Me if I didn't stop I would go completely insane. I ripped the baggie open and dumped out what I had on the ground then went to His house and grabbed My stuff and moved out.

As far as Meth I only had a few more flings with it and that is all.

When the job for the big company was over I wound up working for Jerk #3 doing layout in (some state). The owner of the company was looking for a framing Super and Jerk #3 told Him I would make a good one. $1,000 a week. That job was such a mess. They wanted to roll the trusses on a third floor and I said let Me look at it first, it was a crooked mess.

That job turned into a pain in the ass. There was a Project Manager for the General Contractor that really thought He was the Boss. I had to set Him straight more than once that He is not My Boss. To explain a little about construction, do not tell My People what to do. If You do and it's wrong I have to fix it. They will deny ever telling Your Employees anything. Me and Our Project Manager came back from lunch one day and saw the cornice crew doing something that looked like crap. I asked Them who told You to do that, it was Him of course. I made Them tear it off and showed Them the proper way to do it and then confronted the one that told Them, He wasn't very happy. He did that another time too, both times He was wrong. I really didn't pull any punches with Him when I told Him not to tell My People what to do. As far as those types denying it, that is exactly what happened in (not allowed to say) working for Jerk#3, before I became the Super. Jerk #3 and the Superintendent couldn't find a wall height and I said We have the regular wall height and the truss profiles showing their height, just add the two together. They were both surprised and agreed. When They were done I told Jerk #3 You better get that signed off, He said He trusted the Guy He subbed from. I told Him it's not Him You have to worry about it's that Guy right there in the office. The wall was an inch and a half too tall. When They were discussing it the big Bosses just happened to be there and this Superintendent started saying that wasn't how it was figured out, covering His ass. I was standing off to the side and said that's a lie.

They all looked at Me and Nobody wanted to talk about it anymore. Jerk #3 lost every penny He made on that job because of that and He read the plans wrong for the window layout. At least He fixed it.

Where I was running the job was in (a town), home of (a university) State. It was there that I ran into another drug addict that always wanted to do Meth. Of course He always wanted to get stoned with Me. Kids, that shit is as ignorant as it gets.

When the job in (a place) was finished My Boss sent Me to (somewhere out west) to work on student housing at the (a very beautiful school). He housed Us in downtown (a shitty place). After a week I told Him to get Us out of there, (a great place) was where We moved to. Now there is a nice town.

Another Boss couldn't pass the test to get His license in (a state) so We had to work under the General Contractors license, that was a headache. I was given $35 an hour to make up for it, I paid in $600 a week in taxes. Even the Sub doing the framing was paid through this company. They all got forty hours a week and were working six days a week, They were not happy. I did all of the layout and had to keep an eye on everything. The Guys on the job would tell Me when I wasn't around the crew didn't do anything until I came around, I could never catch Them. When I came around They would holler "Hey Bonito!", meaning pretty Boy.

They knew to keep an eye open for Me. When the job started one of the younger Guys on Their crew said it and I shot Him down, Porque Mi llama es Bonito? He was shocked that I spoke espanol.

I hated that job. We were putting the trusses up on the last phase of it and it was half decked when We figured out the trusses were wrong. No vaulted ceiling, it was a flat ceiling instead. They were going to have Us tear it down until I said no let's put the other trusses next to them and nail them together and then cut the existing truss below the vault, it worked like a charm. This was right after We lost the parapet wall these trusses went next to. It was 50' long and 25' tall at the peak. The crew had it stood and braced but that night fifty mile an hour winds blew it over. There was no way to brace it on the one side except to put a forklift up against it. The Superintendent said when He pulled on the job it was getting ready to fall and He watched it go.

We dodged a bullet at least. From My first day on the site I told the Superintendent and My Boss there is no plan telling Me how I am supposed to build it. On the day of the build I went in and told the Super You know I have been asking and asking for information on this and I have received nothing at all. I then told Him how I was going to build it and He said fine, We underbuilt it. The wind saved Our ass, We would have had to tear it down.

I was glad when the job was over. On My way back to (some state) I went through (a cold state) and helped My Dad celebrate His retirement.

When I did make it back to (some state) I told My Boss I didn't want to run anymore jobs for Him and started doing layout for Him. He then sent Me to (another town) to do a hardware job. Once there I was told by the Superintendent that I was sent out to be the Boss on the job, I quit.

I went to work for the old Superintendent from the job I took over in (a town). Before long We partnered with two Carpenters I knew from My years in (a big city). We were subbing a house together until I got pissed one day and said to hell with it and took off to (a big city). I never had a bad temper as a Child but now it is easy to lose it and just say F it and quit, done it a lot over the years.

I couldn't find anything in (a big city) and took off back to (some city). History was made on that day, that was September, 11th, 2001. I drove to (some city) listening to CDs all the way and then did the same driving around looking for work. It wasn't until I walked into a bar around five that I saw the TV. They were surprised that I didn't know anything about it.

BACK IN (SOME CITY) AGAIN

I'm not really sure what I did once I made it back to (some city). But I wound up building arches on a job in South (some city). Before too long I took over the chimneys on the job and I also built a badass trellis. After a short time I even began doing layout for the same company. When I left (some place) I had My Cherokee, but those things are way too small to run a business out of. I saw a Ford pickup and bought it. Me and that truck saw a lot of miles too.

I was driving it when I found a dead body in (a town somewhere). I was waiting for a Friend to get back from (a town) and was driving around down by a beach. I figured I would collect some shells for a Friend's Daughter. The paper read Sheller finds drowned Fisherman.

I wasn't doing bad at all, but I still had that damn crack cocaine habit. You spend money without even caring to be honest. The crew I had wasn't all that bad. This Fella was a great hand, but He could never cut a board right. Another hand would miss days. And the rest didn't stick around.

I'll tell You how easy it is to make a mistake too. I set up a Kid to cut blocks for the arches, I marked the line to cut them an inch short. That Kid turned out to be a speed freak and cut like an animal all day. I asked if He was checking the measurements but he never did. He wound up cutting a full bunk of sixteen foot two by fours to twenty three inches, an inch short. My fault though. My story when I tell it is that I burned up three board stretchers the next day. When I saw My mistake that night I told the Guys to roll up and while They did I cut a big pile of one inch blocks. The next morning I had Him glue the blocks on to the short ones and I T nailed them. We stretched nine hundred blocks by an inch.

After that work kinda dried up I wound up in (a town) subbing from Fred. The whole time I was subbing in (a city in a big state) I stayed in the same motel room, in (same town) I finally found a place to rent at least.

When I was working on (I am ruining this story by not being allowed to say where) doing Military housing was when the GIs were first deployed to Afghanistan. We showed up the next morning and there were two Labrador puppies following a Chihuahua around. Those two pups had bellies that hadn't eaten for a while, but They seemed as happy as could be just to be out. The Super came up about then and grabbed the Chihuahua and told Us why They were out running about. When the Soldiers are first told they are going to war They have no choice but to throw Their dogs out the door and get on the plane. The dogs are usually picked up by the base dog pound. I went ahead and grabbed the two Labs. No more than I did the Super came back and said His Secretary wanted one of Them and He took the chocolate one. I called a Friend and asked if He still wanted a Lab. That night I took it over and gave Him to His Daughter. I told Her this is not Your Mom's dog and it's not Your Dad's dog, it's Your dog. When the chocolate Lab was taken I said to Him it looks like You just lost Your Buddy, that was His name from then on, Buddy.

"Loneliness will drive You insane", is a fact. When working on base I did something People would call insane. I literally lost My mind one day. I was already crazy, this is hard to admit to, it's true. After that I figured I had better get off base fast, I sold My truck, left My belongings in storage and bought a bus ticket to (a cold state). That move really helped Me get My mind straight. Since '87 I had been losing control, that is a hard fact to look at. People were My main problem, knowing what I know from '63 I saw Them in a different way than They see Themselves. And when They act like They can just do as They please I boil inside, a pure hatred for Their actions. It was coming to a head. Like

I say this move back to (a town in a cold state) actually calmed the Boy down.

When I made My mind up to go to (a town in a cold state) I decided I had better prepare My Parents for what I had in mind. When I was working in (a big city) and staying at the (not allowed to say) I had started doing what it is I am doing right here and now, writing My autobiography. When I was there for My Dad's retirement party I left My memoirs and some tools in His garage. I told Mom to have Dad go find it and to read it, it really didn't phase Them much either.

When I made it to (a town in a cold state) all that I wanted to do was sell My story. I contacted (can't mention the Lawyer) even. All His People do is send You a letter saying something about the statutes being run out. The exact response I received from Them later on from another different time I contacted Him. I also repeatedly contacted (a wealthy man). I contacted (can't say who), (someone) Anybody I thought could help. I tried to hire a literary agent but Their response was that They were confused by Me. I sent Them an unfinished, really garbled, main copy of what I had been writing. It was confusing to say the least.

I wound up buying an '81 pickup off a Cousin's Husband and rebuilt the motor and transmission. I had been working for a company setting up modular homes for a while by then. But after a while People again pissed Me off. I overheard the Foreman of the company say after I left the room "That's the stupid Hand". A few days later He was crawling up a ladder to get on the roof, I jumped at least five feet towards Him. I wanted to kick Him right in the face and send Him back down the ladder. The next day He couldn't understand why I didn't show up to work. I found a job pretty fast too, I went to work for My Boss today.

I messed up some concrete forms working on a hotel My Boss and His Partner were building and knowing how People are about a Kid like Me I said to hell with it and went to (another cold state). I had bought a camper and pulled it behind My rebuilt truck.

I found work fast, it was too easy in (a town in another cold state) to find work then. I worked for this company until the trusses We rolled fell over, the Foreman went up to brace them when We picked up the tools. I found another job the next day. That one I quit because I cut the joist to fit in where another Fella set a beam, He was off on one end. My pay was cut because of it and I quit again. I then went to work for a crew that I was the only White Boy on. I lasted for a while until again I said to hell with Them. My final job in (a town in another cold state) was for a high end framing company. Their Foreman was a Kid that talked down to You, I stopped showing up. They laid Me off They said, hell I quit already by then.

After that (a city) came to mind. I found work but didn't have a crew to take on the job, it was too big to do by Myself. I then headed to (somewhere). Once there I found a job in (someplace I never been), across the river. It wasn't very long and I was Foreman there too.

Things were going well until I went out drinking with two of the Boys on the crew. We were in a bar when an elderly Lady came over and told Me how They were treating Her. I went outside and confronted Them both. Me and one of the Kids came real close to blows but nothing happened. A day or two later I did as I always do when some Kid around Me thinks He can treat Me like shit, I said something in a low kind of a growling voice. My Nephew, the Felon and the nice Guy that couldn't cut know that voice. It means I am getting really tired of a Boy. These two thought They could get Me into a fight after that and took Me out into the hills drinking. One of Them said He was going to throw Me down a hole. I left My leg as straight as an arrow, daring Him to try it.

Nothing happened that night in the hills, but when I showed up to work the next morning They were laughing about it. The Boss came over and said something about it and I said that is it. I dropped My tool belt and walked right over to the same Kid that threatened Me the day before. I have a move where I will walk right up to You and kick You in stride, just like that Fool in (a town I had been in). After I kick You low You will drop Your face down opening up for a spin kick or an uppercut. I started to kick and stopped Myself. He looked at the Boss like what in the hell? When He turned back I hit Him with a right cross. Believe Me when I tell You, I hit that Boy as soft as I could too. I sent that Fool flying through the air. When He landed five feet away I was already on My way, as soon as He hit the ground I came in with a punch intending to do real damage. I never intended to jump and punch Him like that either, it was a reflex. The only thing that saved Him from getting a busted face was that He was covering His face in fear. I then gave Him a few body blows for good measure and then let Him up. That was My last day.

I called one of the big company's Men and He said come to (a big state) He had a job for Me, I was gone. I showed up in (somewhere in the big state) a few days later. I was putting on plywood and gyprock on apartments there. Without a crew I didn't stand a chance as far as making money after the first floor so I went to (a big city). I found just enough work in (a big city) to feed Me. That was when Jerk #3 happened along again. I worked for Jerk #3 doing layout in (a big city) and then the (a town in a big state) near (another big city) for a while.

I went and got a little drunk one night in (a big city) and wound up wrecking the front end of My truck just before that. And then I found out I'm not a Mechanic. When I rebuilt My motor I had an RV cam put in. I had the heads built separately and didn't know You are supposed to put in stronger springs, along with that I put the wrong carburetor on it. Both gave Me fits. I wound up pulling the motor back out and rehoning the cylinder walls because I over fueled the engine by not having the correct springs in the carb. When I was putting it back in the truck I broke the bell housing on the tranny. That was the last straw.

I sold My camper and left all My tools in storage, the ones I hadn't pawned by then, and took off to (can't say where). I was bound and determined I was going to sell My life story. I have always been a Dreamer.

(SOMEWHERE) OR BUST

I drove My truck from (a big city) all the way to (a hot state) before the transmission finally gave out on Me. I then hitched a ride to the next town and bought a bus ticket to (another big city). When I got there I didn't have a clue on where to go so I wound up in (some where). After a week there My pants were literally falling off of Me. I didn't have a belt and was down to change. I would buy a Dr Pepper and some crackers and cheese daily, that was breakfast. Then I walked around looking for work. In the evening I raided an orange tree every night. After a week I put My pack on and started walking. I found an area where there was an abundance of fruit trees alongside the road. I sat there and ate till I was full.

After I walked a few more miles I said to hell with it. I had never even thought about begging before, but I found a piece of cardboard and wrote broke on it and stood on a corner. It wasn't long at all until a young Black Man stopped His car and got out and gave Me a ten dollar bill. The first place I headed for was the (no businesses can be said) across the street. The next thing I did was buy a five dollar day pass for the city bus and got the hell out of the area. I wound up in (a place).

I went to (a place) because there is a (an old dirty magazine) office there, (an old dirty magazine) West. I thought since (somebody) had attempted to contact Me He may be interested in helping that same Boy get His story written. I walked straight up to the office and walked right in, the Secretary was shocked because the door was supposed to be locked. I was asked to leave.

My first day in (a place) I was sitting on the grass in an area that shocked Me at how many Homeless People were hanging out. While sitting there a couple came up and asked If I was hungry and gave Me a sack lunch. It didn't take long to see why there were so many Homeless there. After the next day I knew where to eat three meals a day, more if I wanted to.

This certain Church was the best place for breakfast. If You helped clean up after eating the pastors Wife usually slid You a few dollars. She was supposed to be one of the Children on the show (some show). A truly wonderful Lady. For lunch I found where They gave out sack lunches as well. Then for dinner it was an easy thing to find food at different places. On Sunday You would go to the city hall and a group stopped and fed every week. There were always a few places where You *could shower, do Your laundry or pick up new clothes. I am serious when I say when I first arrived there I was the best dressed Homeless Man around. I had My regular shirts with Me. I always liked wearing a nice shirt. I had a brown Carrhart shirt, a black Remington one and a $70 golf shirt I bought when I was in (a shitty town). One day I hung all My good shirts in a spot I knew Somebody that actually lived properly would find them and take them, they were way too nice for Me anymore.*

I wound up running around with a group of Guys and We were happy just living a life of ease. A two dollar joint was a big thing among Us. There were hard drugs around but none of the Guys I ran with messed with those. I did see a Guy that was a regular around the area once higher than I ever want to be. He came walking onto the (street in a place)moving as fast as He could, sat down by some bystander and rattled off some gibberish and was gone as fast as He had arrived.

What I did mostly everyday was walk. I would go everyday to (another town) and back or else I would travel to another spot just looking around. My second day in (a place) I walked from there to (another place) and back, My feet told the story too. During all My walking I did try and find work though. One day I went up to the top of a hill in (someplace) and found a job I thought. When I called Him back like I was told He had *changed His mind. The same as when I was hired on working on a (not allowed) restaurant when I went back the next day as I was told He had changed His mind as well. When I finally did find a job I was making $15 an hour, rough to live on that there. I started out detaching the trim in a house They were remodeling. Nice place really. You take the 1st pc off and number it one through whatever the last pc is numbered. On the next wall You start with A and finish where the alphabet leadsYou. The next thing I did was to dig a big hole. The drainage in such an old neighborhood was insufficient and to compensate for this any new jobs had to dig a drainage area in Their yard. This consists of a hole around 8x8x8 in the yard. I started digging and had made it about to My waist when the Boss came over and informs Me I had to hand haul the dirt in a wheelbarrow out to a dumpster set up around the corner. It would have been nice to know before I piled it up and had to move it twice. After I had finished that and had the hole probably six feet deep I realized it would have been very easy to have a backhoe come in and have that hole dug in a day. I was already a few days into it. That and dropping the dumpster so far away I said that's it. "Work smarter, not harder" is the saying in the trades.*

I had My guitar stolen a while after I arrived there so on My first payday I went to a guitar store in (a place) and bought a brand new one, with My luck it fell over on Me and broke the neck on it that same day. I went to another guitar store in (some town) and They told Me how to fix it, a pretty easy fix too.

I stayed at what I called the Homeless (ruins it not to be able to say it). I found an empty building, it was right down the street from (an old dirty magazine) West, and I stashed My pack and belongings there behind a fence. I slept sound knowing I was unlikely to be bothered there. My first day there I went around and for about an hour cleaned up all of the trash in the parking lot because I felt it was duty if I was sleeping on the premises

I said that I walked into the (an old dirty magazine) office. Another way I attempted to contact (the Fella that owned the old dirty mag) was I wrote a long letter and dropped it in the mail slot in the office. No luck there at all, it was more'n likely tossed in the trash the next morning.

After around ten months of just being a Bum, I wasn't too good at that, I headed out. I had it in My mind to go to (another state) and see My first great Nephew and His Folks.

I traveled five thousand miles in the next few months.

A LONG ROAD BACK HOME

It took a while before I finally made it to (somewhere in the middle of America). I found out that that area is a strictly Union area and found it tough without a Union card to find any work. My Nephew finally bought Me a bus ticket to wherever I wanted to go, (a city) was where I landed.

My first night in (another city) was an experience. I ran into a Black Fella and ran around with Him for the night. The next day I saw Him again and He showed Me where to find food in town. The Church I ate at one day had the best brats I have eaten to this day. I was not supposed to go back for seconds but I did. There was a Homeless shelter there too that I ate and stayed at a few times. Most Homeless People don't want to stay in a shelter. You have to be in at a certain time of night and You better not have any alcohol in Your system. Most just want to live a freestyle life and be left alone. I have been in and out of the streets since 1980, but I always found a way out.

I even tried My hand at playing My music in the streets of (another city), I didn't do too well. After that I said why not (a famous city)?

It took Me a couple days to hitchhike to (a famous city). Once the Truck Driver I was riding with dropped Me off I made My way downtown. Again I tried to make a few dollars off My music. I could always do good in front of a grocery store until I was run off, but on the strip I made $1. I was playing when a Man and Woman had to stop at a red light while walking down the strip. After listening to Me, He gave Me a dollar. Most People can't really hear You on the street like that so They just walk on by.

After about a week in (a famous city) I said goodbye. I was walking down the freeway with My thumb out when a Man named Lawless stopped and gave Me a ride. He took Me home and I ate dinner with Him and His Wife. The guitar earned Me another ride. His wife had a guitar collection and even tried to buy Mine, of course I refused. I did play at least one of Hers for Them. Then Lawless took Me back to where I could get a ride easily. It wound up having a laundromat there so I did My clothes. I was jamming outside of the store later and the local Sheriff gave Me a dollar.

I made it to (another place I had never been before) a day later and jammed in front of the (can't say the name) there until again told to move on. I did make enough to eat good though. Then I was back on the road. For some dumb reason I headed back to (a city in the middle of America). When I got there My Nephew said He didn't have room for Me. Hell, the way I treated that Boy I understand why. It was raining and I was sitting on the side of the freeway when a car stopped. He said He had gone by and saw Me and swung back. He had a store bought sandwich and a cup of coffee, or a soda I'm not sure which, for Me.

He gave Me a ride all the way to (another big city in the middle of America). Once there I actually went to Church with Him. It was a different type of Church than I had ever seen, a lot of singing and not gospel hymns like You'd think. When We went to His house I met His Friends and showered. Later that evening I went to His Parents house and ate BBQ and drank a few beers with Them. If a Person picks You up on the side of the road it could mean They want sex or to kill You, ot They can just be really nice People.

The next day I was dropped off on the freeway. My sleeping bag was soaked due to the rain so I found an area I could lay it out to dry and I just layed there and soaked in the sun. It took Me one ride to get out of (the other big city in the middle of America) and get to the outskirts where rides are easier. Once there I thought I'd try a Hitchhiker's trick. You make a sign that says You are only going to the next town, it worked.

A Lady Trucker stopped and picked Me up. The first thing You do before You even load Your gear is be honest about it. I told her I was actually heading to (a big state), She gave Me a ride to north of (a big city). After She dropped Me off I used a trick one of the Boys I ran with in (a place) taught Me. Money will blow free until it hits the tall grass, there it stops. I walked alongside the freeway just watching the grass, and $5 was found. I wasn't hungry but I did get a 40 oz beer.

I used to hitchhike that (an interstate) so much in the '80s the rest of the trip until My last ride is not even coming up right now. I do remember what slowed Me down though for a while from hitchhiking so much, it was when I was working for Fred) and taking My vacations like I did that I went through (an area in a big state) a lot using My thumb. One day I was reading the newspaper and there was an article about Henry Lee Lucas and His Pal Otis. They were Necrophiliacs. They would pick up Hitchhikers and kill Them and keep the lower extremities around for Their sexual pleasure. They lived in (a town). That scared Me.

My last ride on that excursion, actually covering five thousand miles, was from a young Lady. I really don't recall where She picked Me up, but when We reached (a city in a big state) She took Me down on (some) street and We drank a few beers. She then drove Me down to an area I knew real well and dropped Me off.

When She left She made sure I had a six pack for the night too.

When I came out of the store after She left there was a Homeless Guy sitting there, He and I hit it off right away. (the Homeless Man) had a camp nearby and We went over there and drank the six pack and then I found My own campsite. I learned a valuable lesson that night, keep your head down. I was right next to a disc golf course I frequented before I left (a city in a big state) the last time and the Prick I was to the nice Guy that couldn't cut it could have been someone I knew that wanted Me to die, or Someone just wanted to kill a Homeless Person. I will elaborate about being a Prick to (an employee), great Guy but He was a Child in My eyes. And I hate the way Children carry Themselves nowadays.

While I was camped? Somebody drove down the road emptying Their .50 pistol into the trees, I found a casing the next morning. When They reached the end of the trees They turned around and did it again. I was laying as flat as possible. You do hear a bullet coming Folks, it makes a sound I can only describe as an angry hornet. When it passes by You know it is within less than a foot away from You.

It took Me a while to get back on My feet but not too long at all to find a sub contract job. My next stop was (some place in the big state).

THE WAY OUT OF THE DITCH

When I started looking for work I called an old Boy I had done some work for just before I dropped everything and headed to (some state). He had a job in (somewhere in a big state). I called a Friend and asked for a ride. If I remember right I had to borrow a saw again too. When I made it there I didn't have enough money to rent a place so I bought a tent and pitched it in an RV Campsite down the road from the job. There was a young Lady there that did the same thing. They stuck Us way in the back.

The Homeless Guy I met after hitchhiking 5000 miles started working for Me, He was an experienced Carpenter. At night after work We would sit outside My tent and take turns playing the guitar, that Boy could play. There was an abandoned camper on the jobsite so He moved right into it too.

I was doing furr downs and punching out and wasn't doing all that bad either. What killed Me was I had money being held until the job was through, I know bad move.

The Superintendent ticked Me off by telling Me to do something that I didn't feel needed done. I was calm at first but then He said do it or get. When I talked to the Fella I was subbing from after I quit He said I didn't finish the project. I think it was around $2,500 I walked away from. You never know about People in the industry, there are tons of Crooks out there, They may have been in cahoots.

I called another Friend and was picked up and taken back to (a city in a big state).

Once I made it back to (a city in a big state) I rented a storage unit and even slept in it until I was caught by the People that ran it, They don't allow such a thing. I then moved to North (a city in a big state) and was working for Jerk #3 again doing layout. I found an area where I could pitch My tent and there were plenty of places to clean up daily after work. It was there that I have quite a few memories, mostly bad.

One day I was sitting in My camp playing the guitar when a Fella came walking into the woods yelling My name. "(My name)! (My name)! (My name)!" was what He was yelling. I looked around and saw Him and not far from Me at all was the Gal with Him. I didn't know what to think so I just sat down and stayed quiet.

Then there was the time I was getting stoned with some Homeless People in the area. This one asked if I had ever had a head job from a Man, of course I refused. I stopped hanging out with that crowd.

One night I walked over to a bar nearby. I was talking to an old Boy and He wanted some Cocaine. I told Him I could find it and We took off to get it. If I remember right something happened to His car only a few miles down the road and I wound up walking back. The thing is I was in an area I knew well, I used to live there before it really turned to crap. (the interstate and a road). I ran into a Fella and He had some crack, I spent the next day or so stoned out of My mind. That was a messed up weekend for damn sure. There was a real pretty Girl that lived right under the (an interstate) bridge. When I was out of money I walked back to where My campsite was, around five or six miles.

This might be when I did My last blast of Meth too. If My memory serves Me correctly. I ran into an old Friend and He took Me out to His house a few times. I was out there with one of Fred's employees, (a goofy Guy), one night and that old friend gave Me a big rail of what is known as Glass. That stuff takes You way out there, I instantly wanted more of it. Even though, I never did any more of the Glass.

About this time I bought an Astro mini van from El Mexicano. The same El Mexicano that Asshole threw out of the bed in (some state We were in). At least now I had a place out of the weather to sleep.

I was contracting some shear wall hardware from Fred then when I was told to get off the job for not having safety glasses on, I was walking across the parking lot. That's how ridiculous it is getting in the construction field now.

I found another job doing the same thing in (some town) and then rented a trailer there. The no cuttin' Son of a Gun started working for Me again. Damn Kid, I had to blow in His breathalyzer to get His car to run. He couldn't function without a beer. Great Guy and I hate to see it. I drink yes, but I do not have to have a beer right out of bed to stop the shakes.

After that I stayed in (some town) for around three years. I used it as a base and worked all over the place. I subbed jobs in (I can't say where). I did the same in (still can't tell You). What killed Me was I would make a bunch of money and be told the next job would start in two weeks, after two or three months You are broke and have a stack of pawn tickets a mile high. Mainly I worked alone, I like to find jobs that I don't really need much help on.

In (a town) I should have been paid for a facial scar I received. I was walking down a hallway with My arms full of tools. There was a broken PVC pipe sticking up and I tripped over it and landed face first on top of My nail gum. I made sure there was a report made in case I wanted to file against it. This job was for Fred. The next job I did for Him was for the same General Contractor. They griped about all of Our safety violations yet the Plumber was allowed to leave full length pipe laying in the halls in which We had to walk on, an accident waiting to happen. That ticked Me off so I said something about My scar on My face, there never was a record of it made come to find out. Plus it was over the time allotted for any settlement the labor board told Me. Fred just told Me They wanted Me off the job after that.

In (another place) I broke My arm when doing the job there. I was getting stoned again, God Damn crack again. I was on the wrong side of town and They knew I usually carried some money on Me, three of them tried to take it. I was so wasted one was behind Me and kept hitting Me on the hinge point of My jaw, trying to break it. I was more worried about the Fella in front of Me. After the Guy behind me hit Me a few times I jumped up and spun around kicking at His leg. I am probably lucky I pulled My punch and didn't kick Him or I would have been thrown into the bayou. After I kicked at Him a really big Fella came running into the fight. Right then I came to My senses, They stayed away from me too. They did not get any closer than twenty feet from Me. It was then that one of the original two started taking things out of My truck bed and throwing them at Me. When He threw the spare air tank I kept in there at Me I was already feeling pretty sure about Myself. When it was about to hit Me I threw up a block and knocked it back towards Him, sending it twenty feet through the air. I didn't know until the next morning I broke My arm right then.

The sad thing about that broken arm is that it was My first and only broken bone. I went to work doing some stairs right after I had it in a cast. I used My arm to push something up after it was in it for a week, it hurt like hell. I had no idea You were supposed to have it reset and let it go. It took Me a full year for Me to work on being able to close My fist. You can still feel the bone where it was never reset. Every now and then it hurts, but I have to live with it I guess.

Now in (another part of a big state) I have at least some good memories. The bad ones of course are due to the Fella I worked for. I had known this Guy since the early eighties. I even ran into Him in (a jail) while I was locked up. I went down there to build stairs and do hardware on a job. After I spent time doing the stairs I found out He had given the hardware to Someone else, it was a really easy job and I would have made a lot of money too. Instead He talked Me into going to work for Him as an assistant Superintendent. I was an Ass. Super/ Security Guard/ Forklift driver on that job. I slept in My truck and used a garden hose to shower, that is until I bought a solar shower.

Our job was right next to a local golf course. It was winter when We started the job and You would see small Alligators out there on the course. My friend even went over and touched one on the tail. I Myself walked over and checked one out, these are around three feet long. When it started warming up the little Gators left and the bigger ones showed up. It was nothing to see an eight foot Gator sitting on the course. One day Someone said there were a couple really big ones seen on the course. I had a few beers that night and went hunting. At first I was standing on the second floor balcony of the apartments We were building and shooting at the big male in the pond around thirty feet away. I hadn't shot skeet until a few years later so I didn't know how to pick Your target and then follow it when You pulled the trigger. I think I must have put five shots into His temple area. I was aiming at His eye and when He moved that little bit my .22 long rifle wasn't powerful enough to penetrate His skull. That's when I got stupid. I went down to where I could get a better shot. It worked though, I hit Him behind the ear. He did a death roll and I was able to see a belly that was easily two and a half feet wide. Like I say, it was a stupid move. Stupid because I forgot all about Her. They were both in there earlier, but now it was just Him. I do believe Animals can communicate mentally because of this. No more than I killed Him here She came. I think She lost contact with him and came to find out why. I hit Her right at the base of the skull making a loud snap and She sank instantly, I broke Her neck.

I wanted to get up early and get the skulls from these two, but it's hard to beat the Groundskeepers on a golf course. They were both gone when I arrived the next morning. They sink for about three hours and then They float to the top I am told.

After that job I ran a job for (some Kid). I believe it was a (can't say it). It is right next to the hospital in (not allowed). After that I wound up back in (a town). By this time I was pretty fed up with working three months and then being off until You were starving. So I jumped into a cab. I drove a cab for a company out of (another town) for ten months, until I was pulled over in My truck and arrested for suspicion of DUI. Can't drive a cab without a license. Driving a cab in (a town) is a tough job. Not dangerous really, just tough to make a living. I averaged $50 a day. $150 was the best day I had and that was when the base emptied out for Christmas break. They let all the Soldiers go at once and You run non stop from the time the base says go. There was one run at night, I was on from midnight till noon five days a week, that some drivers refused. They were scared of these People. All They were were crack dealers, and no I did not know Them. They would take a taxi from the motel to a house and back. All They wanted was to get Their drugs. They sure as hell weren't going to rob You.

One thing I can say positively is that I hadn't smoked any crack or done any meth for quite a while before becoming a cab driver. I have been in (a cold state) for just over ten years at the time of writing this and it was a year

I have to guess before that when I stopped. I have to say I have around twelve years clean right now, I have had the urge a few times but I have never gone back to smoking anything as ignorant as Crack or Meth. One day at a time.

Most of the drivers on Friday and Saturday sat where there were a bunch of bars. You had to wait in a line of cabs. The first in line took the run and the next one moved into position. I couldn't see sitting there for half an hour at least for a five dollar run back to base. I went out to what is known as (not allowed again). If You took Someone to base from there it would be a thirty dollar fare. I would usually get a few that night and then I would head over to where Everybody had been sitting earlier and a lot of times find a flag as it's called around there when all the others had left. I was told by the dispatcher once that in the first three hours of My shift I made more money than the 6 to 6 crews did all day. The reason You really never made money even though it looked like You did was because You had to rent Your cab and give half of Your daily pay to the company plus pay for Your gas. Usually Cabbies don't work it like that and make really good cash. I was driving a cab on (a base), the largest free World base on Earth. That is a big place. When You go to the airport and come in on the Military side You are met by a Soldier with a machine gun in His hands. Same thing if You go to where the Apache helicopters are.

I wasn't on base at the time (I really want to say who) killed those Soldiers, I was off duty. But it sure as hell hit You close to home.

During one of My hitchhiking vacations in the '80s I met up with a Gentleman that had just got out of the Marines. We spent days together hitchhiking. We actually became Friends. He told Me if You are ever around a base and a huge explosion goes off to get to the base. He said it is a Soldier's cry for help. One night while I was in (a town) I was awoken by a huge blast, I shot straight up out of bed. There was a rolling shock wave that hit Me after I sat straight up, I felt five waves from it. I sat and listened for any emergency vehicles thinking it might be an attack. When I heard nothing I figured it was nothing and went back to sleep. At the time I had forgotten what I was told about it. For the next week (a town) was a very different place. At (can't say this one either) the Gal behind the bar had a terrified look on Her face. When I went to (not allowed to say) to go grocery shopping there was a feeling like We were in a war zone. And there were a few older ex Soldiers around that weren't doing anything but watching. The look in the eyes of one of Them told a story. An explosion like that really changes things.

It was at this time I finally realized what happened to My life due to Jerk #2 and Jerk #1. This is when I became one angry SOB.

THEY DID WHAT?

I finally came to the realization that I was screwed with by My old friends. For thirty years I thought I messed My own life up, it was a very rude awakening seeing the truth right in front of My eyes for the first time.

I was watching the late late show one night. When I left the room to use the restroom I heard Him say "Jerk #2, (a town)". Pretty blatant to say the least. I lived at (where I lived) at the time. It was around the same time when I was watching the (not allowed to say). Someone on the show is looking for (His wife) and yells "(His wife)! (His wife)! (His Wife)! Or is that (My name)! (My name)! (My name)!" and shortly after He says "Ah, I wanted the (Unknown) Gorilla". It was said just like when I was living in a tent.

At this time I contacted Jerk #3, Him and Jerk #2 were Friends way before I ever knew the two, I asked Him a few things and He wasn't too interested in being honest. I then went to a tactic I have used numerous times to get paid. You bother that Person so much

They just want to get rid of You and do what You want. It always worked when Somebody I subbed from refused to pay Me what I am owed. I had Jerk #3 so pissed He called Me a braying Jackass. I told Him to have Jerk #2 say I said Eeehaw. One night on a (not allowed to say it) show it was said "Grandpa (My name) says Eeehaw".

I always thought that (an old dirty magazine) was a regular everyday issue, I was wrong. I searched the archives and found the issues from when I was given My (old dirty magazine), they were not the same. There was no "Stoned Hippy" article in those. I contacted Jerk #1 and asked Him about that (an old dirty magazine), He had no recollection of its existence. Lying sack of shit.

I look back at all the acid trips I had taken, not once did I say let's go find some LSD. I was always asked if I wanted to trip. As I have said in this book before, My reply every damn time was I don't know, I guess so. And that is a fact of life.

After learning what had taken place was right before I was arrested while driving cab. I told My Landlord about it and he said I had to move. For the past few years I had struggled to pay My rent every month. I would go by everyday when driving and give Him what I could. I have scars on both arms from selling plasma a few times a week to boot. That is when I said I want

Jerk #2s throat in My hands. I had already lost My truck when arrested because I couldn't afford to get it out of impound. I still had the Astro I bought from El Mexicano so I loaded everything worth anything in it and took off for (a long ways off) again. I made it just a few miles short of (a town) before running out of money. I could have sold stuff and put gas in but I just didn't give a shit anymore. All I could think of was getting to (a place) and just hoping for a chance at running into Jerk #2. I knew He was in (somewhere) actually but I didn't know My way around there like I do in (somewhere). I figured if He was hanging out with those types of People I might just have a chance at finding Him. I made damn sure Nobody knew where I was going, I just fell off the Earth.

It took Me a couple days to get past (a town). After sitting at a truckstop on the eastside of the City I got on the city bus and made My way to the westside. There I had no luck either, You cannot sit on the highway You are lucky if They let You sit at the bottom of the on ramp, hitchhiking is illegal in (a hot state). I finally started walking down a road that ran parallel with (an interstate). I was on the verge of drinking out of an irrigation ditch I was so thirsty when a Marine on His way back to base at (some base) stopped and gave Me a ride. From there I rode the bus all the way back to the (somewhere). There were a couple times I didn't even have the fare and the Driver let Me ride anyhow. It just shows that there are good People out there.

It was different in (a place) this time around. The nice lady from before had passed away and Her Husband was no longer having a daily morning service with breakfast served. I did the same as before as far as walking, I covered a lot of ground keeping My eyes open for a little Prick named Jerk #2.

When You have been in the streets it is easy to fit right in. It took a very short time to be told how to get paid by the state. I went to the DMV and got a picture ID and went where I was told to go. If You fit into what They want You receive over two hundred dollars in food stamps and a debit card for about the same. All You had to do was carry a paper around with You while looking for work and have it signed to prove You are actually out looking. That and sit in a few classes and You live high on the hog. I still have My EBT card too. I didn't know at the time but My Sweetheart lived in the same town where I had to go to do My EBT stuff. I am sure glad She never saw Me there like that.

What I did a lot too was hang out at (a park), it is a chess park right next to the original (a famous place). I got beat a lot but I learned. I would also work out at (a famous place) to at least keep in some sort of shape. But what I did a couple times a day after March 25th 2012 was go to the library. I started a (social media) account and a (another social media) account and told the World what had happened. After a while though I had to stop it on (social media), I wound up having way too many Friends and Family on there to be going on about it.

I went on the internet and found out where the (an old dirty magazine) mansion was. I took a bus to within a mile of the front gate and walked right up to it. When I got there I went straight up to the gate and rattled it, I could have walked right in it was so loose. The security Guards came over the intercom and told Me to please leave the gate alone. I had Them verify that it was indeed the (an old dirty magazine) Mansion and then told Them (My name) is here to see (the owner of the dirty magazine), I wasn't playing either. They just told Me if I wanted to see the Fella that owned the dirty magazine I would have to go through the channels and make an appointment. After I left my timing was impeccable, the bus showed up right when I made it to the bus stop. I am sure the Police were on Their way.

I had made My camp in the exact spot I had before but after a while I had to move on, that is pretty much what made My mind up to leave (a place). I have learned by living like that how easy it is to use the transit system. If You were to do it right I am sure You could go from (some where) to way above (a big city). I took the bus all the way to (somewhere). That is where I started hitchhiking. I figured (another road) would be easier than (a road), I was dead wrong. It took Me a full week to make it to (another city). I did the bus system trick and made My way clean through the City and made My way all the way to (some place) before there were no more buses going east. That was the worst trip I had ever done. Of course if I wound up near a library I would get on (social media). That reminds Me, there was a movie about a little yellow bird that came out after I had been tweeting for a while, I was doing it for ten months at least. On the side of a city bus there was an ad for this movie, this little yellow bird was flipping You off saying "Tweet this". That is the kind of childish and improper behavior Jerk #2 thinks He can get away with.

When I left (a big city) My thoughts were on (where Jerk #1 lives), that is where Jerk #1 lives. I will admit to a few crimes here, the statutes are well over. In actuality I was stalking Richard, and murder was on My mind when I would hit (a state). That week long trip changed My mind. A voice told Me to forget it and I jumped onto (an interstate) heading east instead.

Anybody that lives north of (can't say where) might see My marker. Hitchhikers leave all sorts of writings alongside the highway. I came up with F-in' Heimer was Here. I wrote F-in' Heimer showered here, slept here and other things as well. I am sure some are still visible.

When I made it to (a wild place) I pitched My tent way away from downtown, I do not want to hang out with the Homeless really. I was eating at a fastfood stand and was talking to an old Boy and wound up getting hired, just like the others years before when I called the next day He had changed His mind. What really sucks is that I sold My guitar just to buy tools. Assholes do stuff like that in My opinion. From there I went to (not allowed to say).

I again pitched My tent away from People. There was a spot where You could find work, after a week hanging out with no luck I gave up on that too. That is when I thought why not (a new state for me). The drilling rigs were going crazy then so I set out hitchhiking again. After a few rides I snagged a good one that took Me all the way to (another place in the cold state). When I made (another place in a cold state) I found out where to eat at the homeless shelter. While eating there I was told that the (not allowed to say where) were hiring. A beer runner during shows is the job You want, but I wound up running a window in a food trailer. $50 a day for ten days = $500. A big chunk when You're broke.

You are allowed to sleep in when You are working at the Rodeo, but the day after it's over They throw You out early. I had a few bucks from My tips We were allowed to keep and I stashed My belongings and went walking around downtown. I will never walk by a Jail again and say there's one I've never been in, I went that night. I wound up going to a few bars downtown and got drunk. When I was walking back to My campsite I was pissed off about everything that (Jerk #2) had pulled on Me. Folks I wound up with severe brain damage. I called the Cops on Myself seeking help. I planned on going to (a town), the state hospital in (a cold state), and being checked out. They called Me an ambulance and I was happy as hell just to finally get some help. I was never arrested. While in the ER where They took Me I began to sober up and sat up and told the two Jerks watching Me I just wanted to leave. They grabbed Me and held Me down and restrained Me. Believe Me I wasn't even fighting with Them. Then a female Doctor came in and sedated Me. Next thing I know I am sitting in (can't say it) County Jail. She claimed I kicked Her. Hell I was in restraints way before She even came into the room.

I spent four months in that cell. Everytime I went in front of the Judge He would say "Just admit to it and We'll let You go", I said it everytime that I didn't do anything and back to the cell I went. I had a court appointed Lawyer and it seems She wasn't trying too hard to help Me so I started reading the police report. I found where She said in Her own writing a different story than what She had told the Cops. When I showed My Attorney I was out in two days. When I went in it *was summer, it was -10 when They kicked Me out the door. I made it pretty fast to the shelter and They gave Me some long johns and a good winter coat. One thing I did right before I was locked up was I had My pay-check from the food truck sent to My Parents house, I had My $500 at least. A Cousin of Mine was in (a town in a cold state) when I got out and He told My Mom if I could get to (another town in a cold state)He'd meet Me there with My money and hire Me on, I finally made it to (some place I've never been).*

A NEW BEGINNING

A cousin of Mine was running the company for an old Boy out of (another town in a cold state) in (some place new to Me). It had to have been the easiest job I ever had. It was doing an application in the oil field on big rigs known as a (some company) system. It consists of a plastic can You attach underneath the floor of the rig. It catches the drilling mud that sprays out during connections and is recirculated into use. Most of the time You are on call and don't do a whole hell of a lot, but when the time comes You go out when needed. We were usually at the bar pretty early so We never went out after hitting the watering hole. It paid $15 an hour but housing was paid and You have a company truck to drive. It was pretty easy going really. The most work We actually did was remodel the kitchen.

In a town the size of (some place new to Me still) there really isn't a whole lot to do to be honest. You go to the bar and get drunk and go home to sleep so You can do it again Tomorrow. That can cause issues when You live with People, other Drunks I mean. Myself I didn't really have a problem but (My cousin) and His Nephew had words. I like (My cousin), known Him since '62, but He can be an Ass when drunk. There was an open spot in (the cold state) for the same company and I decided to transfer. That worked out pretty good until Me and the hand I was set up to live with didn't get along, that was after a few months and I went back to (the new place for me). Once in (the new town) My cousin's nephew was talking about "Fucking Everybody up". When I got back from the bar that night He was sitting there and I confronted Him about it. I have been punched before, but after I kicked at His crotch and stopped My foot before I made contact I was punched out pretty good. Not brutal punches, just a lot of them. The way the house was, it wasn't long afterwards that I told (My cousin) off and quit.

I drove around the area looking for work but after a while I headed for (a town in a cold state), back to where it all started. By this time I still had Jerk #2 and Jerk #1 on My mind. I went to My class reunion for the class of '78. The only reason I would even think of going was for a chance that Jerk #1 would show up, no luck there.

I went to work for the same company that the Boss called Me "The stupid Hand". That lasted for a while but I couldn't handle the way things were done and walked off the job. I then hired on as an apprentice Beekeeper. I stayed with it long enough to learn that beekeeping is a pretty tough job. The reason I quit was because I heard the Owner tell Someone one day "He's an Idiot". That boiled inside Me for about an hour before I went and found My time card. I left a message on it after clocking out I am sure He won't forget.

A Friend around town told Me My Boss now had some work going on. I have been with Him for a long time now. I have been His Foreman for quite a spell as well. I have even been the Superintendent for Him on a few jobs. He is pretty much the largest General Contractor in the (a town in a cold state) area.

I am not a racist Person but found it really hard to like His crew. He had built the local (can't mention Them) Casino and Hotel, on a job like that You are required to hire I believe it's seventy percent Native Americans to do the job. Being a White Person You are a minority. I have had to put up with prejudiced remarks a few times from Them. There was one that continually talked back to Me. One day He is taking a scissor lift out of an area I had set it up personally in. It was a small area and there was no reason for taking that lift. When I confronted Him about it He was disrespectful and I bit His head off. It came real close to blows.

I can see where They could have an issue with Me being the Boss. They had been with the company for quite a while. I came in and in less than a year I am the Boss. I really didn't have the experience He had with certain phases of the business, but I have been in the construction field for over thirty years by that time. And a majority of that time I had been a Foreman to boot.

After that I put in My two weeks notice, I think that was only the second one I have ever given to an Employer. I had become Friends with the Guys on the refrigerant crew and one of Them set Me up with a job as the Superintendent on a building in (a new state again). I took off to see another part of the country I had yet to see.

I stayed with that friend (somewhere) an hour away from the job for a while then the Project Manager for the company I worked for told Me the Owners of the building owned rental property in the area. I rented an apartment that was older than Me. It still had an ice box and it had a milk delivery door going into the hall. It was nailed closed of course so Nobody could crawl into Your apartment. I paid $800 a month. No deposit, and I never paid any bills. The sad thing is the apartment was located in the heart of (somewhere), a very, very Gay area. I would do a lot of walking and going to any bar I found that wasn't a flagrant Gay bar, I found three in the neighborhood I would even venture into. During Their Gay Pride parade, just a few blocks away, I went to (another town) and spent the day. This is the exact *same area that was overrun recently and held by those Hoodlums, the one right next to the Police Station.*

The job? I was I think the fourth or fifth Superintendent on site. The last one was a Friend of (a Friend) and had Him bring Me in so He could quit. That job was a disgrace. It was called an apodment. The kitchen is on the first floor and the rest of the five floors are efficiencies. It was actually broken up into five different sections where You had five different kitchens in the building. The first floor was being finished when I arrived. When I went and looked at it I really couldn't believe how the integrity of the building was already a disgrace. On the first floor over a six foot window They had a flat 2x4 header in, unheard of. The walls were only eight foot tall with the height of the window sills there was no way in hell You could put a load bearing header in the wall. In the first place with that much weight on top of it a 2x8 wall would be more sufficient. I made the Carpenters doing the floor system double the rim joist over the windows and hanger the joist. I still don't think it was structural enough really, but the job really should have been rejected from the City, there were no structural plans period. It was a design builder that had a Buddy of His stamp His Engineer stamp on the plans and they passed.

The job was in a narrow area and You could no way get a forklift or a crane on site to handle material. The

Framers had to build it in layers and hand hauled every bit of wood, sheetrock for firewalls and plywood for the walls and floors by hand, every stick. And to top it all off the Kid that drew it would not agree with anything. He said if I drew it it will work. I stayed long enough to see the roof decked and I quit.

I went straight back to (a town in a cold state). After a week waiting for a call I finally went back to work for My Boss now. I didn't miss a beat and went right back to work in the same position and pay rate.

IN AND OUT OF TOWN

I made it back to (a town in a cold state) and We finished the job I was on before I left. After that there was a rumor about being laid off. I have been with this company long enough now to know that didn't include Me, of course I was clueless then. I had a Friend in (a new state to Me) that had talked to Me a few times about coming out and joining the Union so I took Him up on it.

I was able to get into the Union easily enough once I told the Representatives how long I had been a Carpenter, They made sure I had My card right away.

I was able to get hired on with the same company My Pal was working for and I thought I was doing alright too. One day He came over and told Me They want Me to button My shirt up, I just never felt comfortable with the top button hooked. I wasn't trying to be cool or anything like that either. One day on the elevator going back up after lunch Someone riding up said "Button that shirt Mister". Like I say I never thought anything about it. Kind of rude to tell a Person something like that in My opinion. One day after working a week They said that the job was caught up and laid Me off.

It took Me a week to find another job through the phone connection You are given through the Hall. Once I was working with this Fella and He always said "That Weirdo shit" when I was around, I didn't last long there either. The only good thing about the whole (a state) experience is I did receive a certificate stating I am a trained scissor lift and boom lift Operator. I said to hell with that place, the main reason I wanted to go there was I had yet to see that country. I made a call to (a state) and had a job before I hung up.

I went to work for a Fella as a Foreman instantly. I worked for Him for a long time too. On one job it was right around the corner from the job I was Superintendent on not long before, I have to say I think it was nearly a year since I had left and They hadn't even set windows on it yet. I am sure the inspectors were not friendly. I did just recently contact the Gentleman I was working for and told Him They should sue the City. A five story building with only one staircase is not an acceptable fire escape. If You are on the fifth floor and the fire is closing the stairs You are dead unless you jump. As I said before, that building should have never been passed by the City planning Commision.

I didn't really like the thought of being back in the area, I am used to cities but You can keep (a city). It was nice when We went to (another nice town) on the eastern side of the mountains. It is a very small town on the banks of (a beautiful lake). We built the lower part of a house for a Fella that owned a Union plumbing company and a bar in (another nice town). We built the basement part of the house and the upper part was something new to me, SIPS panels. They are plywood exterior with foam filling, actually pretty structural. We spent most of the winter on that house too. I really liked (another nice town) and even thought about staying there. The People were friendly and there seemed to be enough work to keep Me busy.

After We finished the house in (another nice town) We went to an even smaller town, (can't say where). I had been to (can't say where) once before. See in (can't say where) on Memorial day and Labor day They have the biggest flea market You will ever find I am sure of that. The food vendors were so exceptional I spent more money eating different foods than I did on any items for sale. When We made it to (can't say where) We did a torch down roof system on a shed and re-roofed the house that used to belong to My Boss and His half Brother's Dad. His Brother was the one that first talked Me into going to (a state) before I quit My Boss now.

These two and others had done so much work around the place I was impressed. They took old pull behind campers and took off the axles and set them on a solid base. Then They went inside and stripped them out and made two bedroom sleeping quarters out of them, a really nice set up. When the (can't say where) flea market was going on They have a packed house there. When I first went to the flea market I knew of the place but never found the turnoff, I drove past it at least twice. (can't say where)is the type of town where Elk walk right down the main street. There is a picture You may have seen where the Elk are eating hay right off a semi, I guarantee it is in (can't say where) for certain.

After We left (another nice town) and (can't say where) I had a tough time finding a place to live. I started renting a motel when I could but mainly stayed in the truck. I was making $30 an hour but spent it too fast. Me and one of the Hands, hung out at the some Casino in (a town). They had cheap beer and good food. The both of Us had Our trucks parked in the parking lot next to the Casino. I lived like that for a couple months. As I have said before I can always find a place to take a shower. I would either go to (another town) and go to a center where I could shower for free or I had a spot where I found a spigot where Nobody could see Me. It's tough but Ya gotta stay clean.

Then one day We were working on a burnt out building and the Boss and two others tore a wall down right next to Me without warning, that pissed Me off.

When You are working on something that can fall over and kill You let People know what's going on around Them. It pissed Me off so much I told the Boss off and got in My truck and left. A few days later My life fell apart again. I was actually just screwing around. I wasn't really looking for work or doing anything constructive. Actually I was hanging out in a Casino trying to make some money off the little bit I had. I wasn't winning and thought I would go down the road and buy some pot and then come back. After doing so and getting high I was going to turn into the Casino and another car was turning and I had to slow down. It was a blind spot I was sitting in. A Fella came flying over the hill and I never saw Him coming. It was in a forty five mile an hour speed zone and He left around a thirty foot skid mark, He sure as hell wasn't doing the speed limit. He hit Me so hard it knocked the breath out of me and made Me discombobulated on what was actually happening for a few seconds. When I figured out what had happened My first thought was scary, I thought a Family might have just hit Me. I motioned for a Witness to come over and He cut Me out of my seatbelt. The first thing I did was check on the other car, I wasn't too damn worried about Myself. Two state Highway Patrol officers showed up to the crash site. The more experienced Officer after My truck was on the wrecker asked how I was getting home, before I could answer the younger Officer came over and got in My face. "Have You been drinking?", of course I was honest and said I had drank a few beers. Like I said, the wise Officer knew I was a long way away from being drunk and was telling Me to get home. When I asked the younger Officer about the skid marks He said, "I'm not worried about Him, I got You"

This Kid put Me in His car and made Me sit there in sweltering heat for quite a spell. Finally I told Him this is kind of cruel and unusual punishment isn't it? When He asked Me what I meant I showed Him I was drenched in sweat and He rolled down the window probably about an inch. I then looked at Him and asked Him, You're what about 25? When He said yes I asked Him straight out of the academy aren't You? When He again said yes, I said it shows.

When I went to Jail after the blood test I was forced to take I was being processed in and the Jailer asked if I felt like hurting Someone or Myself. Being a bit pissed off I said Ya I am. They put me in the funny ward. You wear a smock and that is it. No blanket, no pillow, nothing but the smock. It wasn't My first time wearing the piece of crap either. When I went to (some) County Jail before I went to (a jail) I was in a holding cell and had made a makeshift knife out of a plastic spoon. I had it up to My jugular and was trying to find the courage to push it in and end My sorry ass life when a jailer looked in. They put Me down with the Hard Cases and Crazy Bastards. You wear the same smock.

After I convinced the Doctor in (a state) that talks to You I wasn't going to kill Myself I was moved. Then I was let out on My word that I would go to court. I went to a (not allowed to say where) rented a room and went out and bought a bottle of (whiskey) and a bottle of sleeping pills. Before I went back to the room I saw a Homeless Man and gave Him $100 and said He needed it more than Me. I then downed the pills and the whiskey, I woke up with a pissed soaked bed because My bladder opened up and let out every bit of liquid I had in it out, the mattress was ruined. The next day I left the motel and even bought a pack of razor blades to finish it but couldn't do it again.

Right before I said goodnight I put on (social media), Goodbye cruel World, and went to sleep. It really freaked My sister out. She put a missing Persons report out and did anything She could to find Me. It was late in the day when I finally found a phone cord at a store and charged My phone that I saw what She was doing. I called My Bud in (some state)and my Nephew both and explained what was happening, I cried hard for both of Them.

I told My sister I really needed to go to the Mental Institute and get My head straight so She tried to get me in. From what She told Me They didn't think I was that bad off. So Mom found a (some) Church that would take me in, They were in (clear across the country). I was on the (somewhere). My sister bought Me a bus ticket and I was out of (that state) never to return if I could help it.

COAST TO COAST

After attempting suicide in the manner I did You are very shaky when it comes to standing. I would have to keep Myself from falling over. It was like that all the way to (some state) and then some.

I have to admit saying something like I attempted suicide is a harsh thing to mention. But the life I have lived is nothing but one painful experience after another. To be straight forward about why I tried to end My life, I wanted to get (My true love) out of My mind. The love I feel for Her is astounding. I have heard the saying that Somebody met another Person and felt like They knew Them for all of Their life, I really did feel that way about My true love. I have thought of Her and a very warm feeling has swept through My body. True love is a wonderful thing to experience, even in Our case. It is a feeling that will not leave Me for the rest of My life.

When I did make it to (a state) I was told by the (some) Church that in order to stay with Them I had to abide by Their rules. One rule was that if speaking to another Member of the Church You spoke of nothing other than the Lord. I decided They were going a little overboard on that just a bit. You could not speak of anything else? That is absurd. I said I couldn't see things in the light like they expected and started walking down the road with My thumb out. I can't remember exactly what towns I made it to in the next twenty four hours, but when I did make it to a bus station and get a ticket out of the south I was still very unstable on My feet. I stood for over a week making sure I didn't fall over, that is a memory for Ya.

When I made it to Iowa I was pretty damn hungry by then. I found out where the Homeless shelter was and made a beeline for it and was given a sack lunch during a layover. When You have lived in the streets You learn how to find food fast. The only other part of the trip that sticks out was being laid over in Radar O'reillys hometown, I thought it was neat. After a few days on the bus I finally made it back to where I have been since, (a town in a cold state). I stepped right back into My job like nothing had changed.

Dad helped Me find a vehicle and I paid Them back for it. It wasn't the GMC 4x4 I left in, but it was transportation. I am nearing the end of My autobiography, but I am not quite finished. I still have the past six years to talk about, and they were not a breeze either.

THE FINALE

Life in (a town in a cold state)? I have lived in the same apartment from right after I made it back from (a state). It is so small that half of My front room is full of tools. I should get a storage unit but then I would have to go find what I need instead of looking across the room.

I have been in the position of a Foreman for a General Contractor here in (a town in a cold state) for close to a decade now. I started My resume with the company by cutting in a seven pitch roof for the Bosses Son before I was ever made El Jefe Grande. Since then I have supervised a few jobs and have been the Boss just under another Boss.

Life as a Boss in (a town in a cold state)? I mentioned the Kid that was taking My lift, a Native American. He is a top Hand too. But He began talking shit again on a job for the Tribe. He confronted Me about the racial statements I was putting on (social media), in which I never posted. I calmed Him down after a spell. The only thing I would consider racial was a joke I reposted. In the first place He is not a Friend of Mine on there so it would be hearsay. I told the Bosses Son and He talked to Him was all. Then not long after that He was talking garbage to Me, actually mocking every word I said one day. I wrote Him up on the office email, He is no longer employed. That is really too bad, He actually is one of the best Hands in the area.

Getting back to when I first showed back up here in (a town in a cold state). I drove My Jeep Cherokee for a spell until I bought the '99 Tahoe I have presently. I sold the Jeep for about what I paid for it so I did alright. And then I tried to renew My DL.

When I went to renew My drivers license I was refused because of what happened in (that state). That hit Me hard due to the fact that I really didn't do anything serious to begin with. It was around a week later I said enough again, I put a gun to My head.

I say I put a gun to My head, and yes I pulled the trigger too. Yet I lived. The gun is a black powder .36. I know for a fact I can load a pistol, but there was no powder in it to project the ball into My cabeza. I have learned since then that just the cap will push the ball into the barrel. The next night I tried it again, this time it had a full load of powder. The problem is that the ball from the first shot was lodged in the barrel and stopped the second shot from killing me.

Jerk #2's Pal is a gun geek and lives in town, My

place I have broken into with a plastic card. Just speculating on how My powder disappeared.

With the two attempts to end My life going bust I said one more. I took 100 sleeping pills and crushed them into powder and mixed them in water and drank them. I finished half a fifth of (whiskey) before I passed out. The next thing I remember was trying to get out of bed and peeing uncontrollably. I vaguely remember being revived in the front on My house in My boxers. Then a Lady Officer was putting the bottle of (whiskey) in front of Me asking if I wanted anymore.

The only clear memories are hallucinations. After all the drugs I have done in My life I had to almost die to actually hallucinate. I woke up after seeing all sorts of things, on the bathroom floor cowering. I could not walk, I had to drag My sorry carcass across the floor. When I came into the kitchen I looked at My two recliners in the other room. One had a Man sitting in it and the other a Woman, I do believe still that They were Police Officers. Neither looked at Me and They never said a word to Me. One of the things I remember was when it all started My Boss showed up and said leave Him alone. I took it as He was being mean. At one point I came crawling out of the bathroom and My Boss was sitting in My chair, the next time I came out He was gone. That made Me grab the end of the counter and pull Myself up. Again when I came into the room He was sitting there and I told him I got My ass up. I gave Him a hateful look because I thought He was out to ruin Me from the hallucinations I had earlier. In reality My Boss made Me come back to reality.

After that I thought the Cops were outside My door. A knock on My door and I answered and the Cops stated They were going to kick My door in if I didn't open it. When I did there was Nobody there. There was a Police tape in the backyard too. I lost so much control I ran to My neighbor's house in My boxers looking for help. I talked to Her later and admitted it all, sorry to say. What can You do when You are beating on Someone's door nearly naked? That was around three years ago.

So maybe You can see why I want to give up, or more importantly why I need to thrive. I have been through hell and returned only to go through it again and again. I sure hope what I have written has opened eyes and minds. In the first place, leave lonely People alone. They already hate life and You make it worse. No Grown Adult being Male or Female will antagonize a lost soul and that is a fact of life.

I have breezed through this whole book with such a fever that I have had to go back and write special sections of what I remembered later, instead of rewriting the whole story again. I will print those sections after this final page, which I am pretty sure I might have to add on to as well.

With this all said I will bid you a partial farewell, I will add a note at the end as well. I just want People to understand that this actually is My life as I live on this day of September 17, 2022.

Again, KIDS DO NOT DO DRUGS!!!

FORGOTTEN, THEN REMEMBERED

(just add ins from parts I forgot really)

This chapter is set up just for those tidbits I forgot in other chapters. Like I was a bedwetter until I was in junior high. My Parents even had a Man come by and sell Them an alarm system that finally broke me. It was an electric pad that as soon as it was wet woke the whole damn Family up. Parents teach Your Children that if They have to pee pinch Themselves. When They do have the pee dream They will wake up on time. I still have that dream, as soon as the stream starts I wake up though.

Another thing that happened in 1981. When I was in (a town)Me and My Uncle were watching TV. He was flipping through the channels and (a big time show host) came on. He changed channels and then went back to (a big time show host). When He flipped back (a big time show host) said "The Weirdo" and He knew

I was watching and He went blank. They had to go to commercial. When He came back He was quoting (a rock band). In those days TV was strange to say the least, Aye? I can gauran fucking tee I felt like a Man right then and there too.

Back to the Child in '63. These are things I didn't get written before printing that chapter. It is easier to continue in this manner than to rewrite the whole thing. "A Man has nothing to prove", "You're never as Grown as You think You are", "You are getting too big for Your britches", "There sure are a lot of Kids", "Severe mental problems", "There's a method to My madness", "Sarcasm is youth", "I guess She told You, didn't She", "The Girl's insulted", "I know how to treat a Lady". I am positive there is more I can add, but I have to end this story sometime and I feel it is now.

To prove My honesty I have to admit to some things I would rather forget. I told you about kissing that Teenager and jumping up and practically running out of the room, Her name was (cannot mention Her name I am told) I remember. One of the worst memories I have comes from the same year I had My Sweetheart fall in love with Me for the second time. My sister was having a tough time making ends meet being a Mother of two and divorced. Her Kids were living with My Parents same as Me. One day, I really don't know why I never asked the Girl to do so, She sat on My knee. I put My hand on Her knee. When I did, Her Brother is a Witness, I stared with My eyes bulging at My hand wondering what in the hell was going on. She said something about My hand and then I looked at Her Brother with a look that said it all, written all over My face was, what did I just do? Her Brother is a tough Kid, if He thought I was needing it He would have whooped My ass the last time I saw Him for it I am sure. My hand on a knee? I have memories. The first time I met a nice Gal, She turned out to be a good Friend of My Sweetheart's later, We were at a party. She happened to be sitting next to me, I put and kept My hand on Her knee. She never said to move it and I even gave Her a ride home that night with no expectations involved. When I was first alone with My Sweetheart? With shaking hands I say. Then there was the time in (an old bar) I was sitting with a Gal I was trying to get to know, She just removed my hand for Me. Damn retarded Son of a Bitch anyhow.

This is one that really disturbs Me. I was sitting on a foot rest when Jerk #1 and Jerk #2 both got real close to Me. This was before I hit Jerk #1 with His guitar. One in the front and the other to My rear. I had a very strange feeling come over Me, it is really creepy when I look at it now. I can say without a doubt They were thinking of My behind. I know it is strange, but all of a sudden I thought of My ass. Jerk #2 is a game player that really thinks He's too big to fail. I see Him now.

One thing I remember about this Boy Jerk #1 is that when We worked together as after school Janitors at an Elementary He would always set it up to where He would jump out at You in different areas and try and scare you. He also knew how to steal from the school, sneaking food out of the pantry and getting free sodas and the likes. I really wish I had never met the piece of crap to be honest.

Here is one I really cannot believe I didn't put in before. This was when I was working for an old Friend, before I moved to (a big city) in '95. It was at another one of those large (a big state) dance halls when I was walking around. I looked at this young Lady and saw the most beautiful face You can imagine. I had to stand there and look at Her for a few moments. I then continued to cruise around the place. When I made it back around, I was about thirty feet from where I first saw Her, I was just standing there taking it all in. Low and behold this Kid snuck up behind me. This drop dead gorgeous, the most beautiful Gal on the face of the Earth, in all reality, walked up behind Me and put Her breast right in the middle of my back. I went into shock instantly. In actuality it pissed Me off though, I stood there and ignored Her until She walked away. Boys and Girls, I had a Grown feeling too. After a minute I walked back by where Her and Her friends were and did the same thing, I looked at Her in astonishment. I made another circle around the place and then came back, this time I was heading straight towards Her. That was when I was stopped by a Bouncer. I wound up even going to Jail that night for refusing the cab the Cops outside offered. Hey, I have the World's worst luck and that ain't no doubt. Again as with Nancy I never even thought about checking, or posting, an ad in the classifieds. I am Dumb.

My last memory of doing any Meth is vague. I have done some with (some Kid I knew), the Girls Dad that I gave Buddy to. And then there was the time with another Pal, that one surprised Me. That old Pal and Me drank heavily together for a while years before but I never knew He got stoned until that night. Other than that I can only guess that at the time of writing this it has been around thirteen years since I have had any of that trash around Me.

I have a memory that is very dear to Me. I was sitting alongside the highway during one of My hitchhiking vacations when a bus load of Elderly People went by. I made eye contact with a Lady on the bus, She had love in Her eyes. I have seen it four times including this time.

A memory I wish that never took place? I was molested by (My sister), I guess You can call it that. She had Me feel Her up, quite often too. I wasn't allowed to take My clothes off though. That right there says that I repressed every memory of her yelling at me. I would have never gone along with it if I had any recollection of the brutal abuse I took from Her. When I see how the Girl is, and I mean Girl even at the age of around 65, plus how She was as a Child I feel a rage inside. It is no wonder the Family rarely sees her. Mom and (another sister) both say after being around Her for a short spell They've had enough of Her.

In 1980 a new law came out, the Civil Service law. Jerk #2 and Jerk #1 told Me They went and signed up, I never knew what it was even about. One thing about Jerk #2 is He went around saying He "Wasn't going to go to Afghanistan and fight for oil". It was just like most things in My life, right after they happened My mind just blocked them out, I never thought about it again until the mid '90s.

I mentioned working on (a base) and doing something I think was insane. I should have been locked up for the way I was for years. I was so bad off that during My time in (a big city) I would get so angry at Someone, especially on the freeway, I would pull up next to Them and start yelling. Yes I was a totally messed up individual. I hated life like most will never understand and it was eating Me up inside. I still have anger, but I am no way on Earth the way I was in the past.

When I was living in (a town) I drove to (another town) everyday. I was building arches and doing stairs for an old Boy. His payroll Gal kept screwing with My pay so I was unable to really get anything going money wise. On some nights I would just sleep in the truck instead of driving the seventy or so miles home. And when I did go home I didn't have any hot water, a shower in that place would make your head hurt it was so damn cold. I decided not to even try for a while longer than I should, without cleaning up I stunk. I literally smelled like shit. When I noticed I said to hell with it and took the coldest shower I can remember. Even a Whore bath is better than going without, before long You really cannot stand Yourself.

I told You about living with four Girls, always being verbally abused. It was after We had moved back to (a cold state) when all four of Them were doing something in the kitchen. I walked in and was actually being nice to Them when My sister started yelling at Me again, I didn't stand there and take it this time like all the other times. I said something back, pointed My finger at Her, and walked out. We were into CBs at the time and as soon as I sat down in the chair in the living room She ran in and got on the CB yelling "He's beating Us! He's beating Us!!". I just sat there and remained calm. When Dad walked in I sat up planning on telling My side of the story when I saw a fist coming from left field. Me and the chair went backwards and I went out the back door. Once outside I stopped and asked Myself where

I was going to go. Mom then came out and talked to Me and that was the end of it. Years later I was riding with Dad somewhere and I mentioned it to Him, I cried when I told him I never hit those damn Brats.

Some People I knew. Two Brothers. One has been in and out of mental institutes since 1980. He showed up on (the street I lived on) with some Guy that broke out of the (another big city) mental hospital with Him. One day He told Fred He was going to go weird out. He wound up getting His picture in the (a university) paper after He crawled up a tree naked on campus that same day. The Guy just did things to be crazy in My opinion. When We were working on (a base) right after My Nephew came to work He was around Us. He refused to ride in the cab of My truck, He wanted to ride in the back. At stop lights He would stand up and grab My roll bar and shake the truck acting all wild. (a Man) let Him stay at His house until He was out in the yard spraying water into the air from the garden hose and running around the tree at two in the morning. I went and told him to get His crazy ass inside. Soon after He was riding in the truck when I saw Jerk #3 broke down on the freeway and stopped. He jumped up and started His act in the back of my truck, this time it pissed Me off and I yelled at Him to get His ass down. He jumped out of the truck and I haven't seen Him since. If You have ever seen the (some food chain) commercial where the

Guy at the end shoots the fire extinguisher at the other Fellas crotch, I guarantee You that is this Fella being sprayed. Look at the hair at the beginning of the commercial, all nice and neat. At the end the same Fella has greasy hair, that's Him. I tried quite a few times to help the Kid out but He just doesn't give a damn it seems. He is a real close personal Friend of Jerk #2's so I am sure He just acted like He did around Me to bug Me. Jerk #2 is a big time game player. And then You have the other Brother. One night I was asleep in My waterbed when Someone hit the mattress really hard. I came up with My foot cocked ready to strike, there's this Kid standing there naked with a stupid grin on His face. I said You'd better get and He got. One morning I heard Him talking to a couple I allowed to stay there. He was lying through His teeth about Me for some reason. I got up out of bed and went into the other room and told Him I think it is time to move out. I gave Him until the weekend. Come Friday He gives Me His rent like everything was fine. I told him I am serious and He needs to get His stuff and leave right now. He went into the other room and after a while I went to say something to Him and He was putting a .38 up to His head. (the Gal living there) just got out of the shower and I told her to talk to Him. Before long She came out with the gun and gave it to Me. He moved real soon too. Then one day He came back with another gun wanting His .38. Jerk

#3 was there and didn't allow Him to take it because (the other brother) owed Him. I called the Cops and had His sorry ass arrested. At the Police station I could hear Him talking to the Cops, He was telling a pretty tall tale and I asked Jerk #3 who was sitting with Me, You hear those lies? He went quiet and soon the Cops told Us just to go home, He was convicted of a felony. Do not pull a weapon on Me I will not be polite. One funny thing about these Brothers is that all of a sudden Their Mom became very wealthy.

The way My home life was is ridiculous to say the least. My two older Sisters bought Me a (a rock group) album for my birthday one year. I was listening to it and Mom said turn it down so I did. She then came bursting into My room, grabbed the LP and threw it against the wall yelling "I said turn it down!". After some thought I made My bed up like I was asleep and put on My long johns and grabbed some things and was about ready to crawl out the window when She came in and saw what I was doing. You better believe I was running away. Jerk #2 was a runaway Himself. His Dad wouldn't let Him get a drivers license, I really doubt if His life was tougher than that.

I do have a record with the Police. On one occasion I was charged with a Terrorist threat. I didn't do as I was charged. I was in (another town in a big state) drinking in a bar. I was bought a shot and as soon as

I drank it I knew it was time to leave. When I got up to leave I knocked a table over with a full pitcher of beer sitting on it, I grabbed the table before it hit the ground and stood it back up while only spilling a couple drops, that's how fast I move. When I went outside there was a Fella there that I had been talking to before in the bar. I was mad because His Friend inside earlier sounded Gay and I mentioned it to this Guy and He said that was His Friend, I put both of My fingertips at His throat real fast and said You don't want to mess with People. That was when the Bouncer came out and got into a fighting stance. I told Him You never know when Somebody is going to go to Their car and get a gun and come back. I then turned and walked away, I heard Him coming from behind and never thought about getting out of the way and He tackled Me and held Me down until the Police came. When I was in Jail I said to hell with this life and tied My shirt to the bars and knelt down attempting to hang Myself. You would really want to end it bad to kill Yourself that way, after I began choking I had to stand up. When I went to court the Assistant DA told the Judge that I was told to leave the bar twelve or thirteen times. I said that's a lie and nothing was done, I was convicted. Yes I was an ignorant Drunk that night for certain, I was definitely in the wrong but I sure as hell wasn't told to leave at all, I left on My own.

This is where I have to stop.

THE REST OF THE STORY

(some more crap I remembered later)

I have everything ready to mail My story into the Library of Congress in order to receive My copyright, but I keep remembering things I haven't put in it yet. I guess I'll just have to add in another chapter especially for these. Here We go.

I was hitchhiking home from a (a real badass guitarist) concert in downtown (a city in a big state) when I was given a ride by two Fellas. On the way They were talking about some Black Guy trying to hit on Them all night. They were definitely Homosexuals. I just sat in the back and listened. It had been a seriously long walk already before They stopped and picked Me up and I really didn't feel like walking too much more. When they turned off of (can't tell You) and let Me out, the Passenger leaned on the car door and told Me They'd be back in a half hour to see if I was still there. It was a reflex to side kick him right in the mouth. I'm not positive but the way I kicked Him, and He never had a chance to move, I am sure I jarred His teeth loose if not knocked them down His throat. That Gay stuff is not tolerated by Me at all, fact. As I say, it was a reflex. I did not intentionally go out of My way to hurt this Fella.

My Bud across the street in junior high always had a thing for My sister. I had a crush on My oldest sisters soon to be sister in law as well. One night My Sister and Her asked Me and My Bud if We wanted to play strip poker, I backed down. He didn't hang around Me too much after that if My memory serves Me right. One thing about Him, He was a little Pervert I have to say. He wanted, and I allowed, to poke holes in the bathroom ceiling so We could look at the Girls. We had a great advantage spot, We built models in the attic all the time so We were always up there.

A continuance from 1963 would be, "It sure doesn't make Ya feel much like a Man". Did I mention this one from around seventh grade? "I wasn't Man enough to hold Her in My arms".

I did mention that I worked at (a pizza place) and when Our shift was over on the weekends We already knew where all the parties were at. Most of the time the parties were in one of three locations then. (a party spot) was the most popular. Then there was (a party spot) and (another party spot)l. If You were (where Us Kids drove regularly), as We did in the seventies, and it was empty You headed to one of the three and You would usually find a Kegger. I really should have had My drivers license taken away from Me in high school too. My Parents knew what I was doing, but if They knew that most of the drives home were in a blackout it would have ended. In a normal Family I would have been grounded fast. Plus I had a lead foot and the Cops knew Me pretty well, nowadays with the speeding tickets I was getting on a regular basis They would have yanked My license fast.

I walked past an elderly neighbor Lady when I lived in (some place I lived). After I said hello She said while walking off, "There's nothing wrong with a Man".

I was standing in a bar in (a bar district), a bar district in (a big city), when a Gal walks up to Me and takes My beer away from Me and asks, " Are You always this boring?", and then drags Me out onto the dance floor. Once We started dancing She asked Me if I could dance dirty. I had Her melting against Me. I was about to compliment on Her dress and proceed to seduce Her when one of Her Friends came up and gave Her a cell phone telling Her She had a call. The rest of Her Friends were standing there after They left looking at Me like I did something wrong. Hell, She instigated it. I really cannot win.

I had better end this or I will go on for way too long. As a final note though I will add two things. "The Kid's mature" is actually a Smartalleck. And the name is not (still can't say My name) it is (can't say My name). I want the Mick reinstated into the name. According to Dad the Irish cut out the O' and the Mc to be accepted in the 1800'. (nope, can't say My name) sounds retarded, it's (ruins My story not being able to say My name).

WHAT I HAVE LEARNED OVER THE YEARS

Like I say, I literally became that Fool from the "60's. At first I was just a Kid that Somebody was messing with, and then I became this mind. Then I remembered 1963. That turned the Child's life around in another way all together.

The sayings I have learned just by being this Kid are, "A Kid's a Kid, I know I am one", "Who in the Hell would call that a Man ?", "Just another Kid", "Don't tell Me what to do!", " If You had a Man You'd be mature", "Men will make You mature", "I am salt of the Earth", "I don't need a Girl", "I'm a Kid too", "Children do this", "I'm a Man", said sarcastically, "A Girl's a Kid", " God Damn Love", "Need's a Kid", "I'm not a naughty Boy", "This old Boy grew", "I'm an old Man". One of My own is, the first thing You do is admit to it. "I grew since then", "And then They expect to be called one", "Mr. Man", "Boy's make Your Girls mature", "Shit stinks", "You're not Man enough to make Your Girl mature", "Don't laugh Boy",

"One Man Everybody knows", "That is one", "If You had a Man You'd be mature", "The Boy can shave, now he's a Man" again said sarcastically, "A Man is a Man!", You just grew", " I'm the only Man around here", "I kick the shit out of that Woman", and His Wife sat there as a Woman afterwards, "The word is mature", and "The word is Man".

It is just like I say about the things I learned at the age of three, there is more I am sure but I cannot remember them all at this time. I feel I have said enough as it is too. I really have to stop and see about getting this published.

LIFE AS A SPACE CADET

After I read that (an old dirty magazine) My mind changed, in reality I became that Kid I saw in the sixties. It was a year or so later when I remembered what happened that year before I started school. The main reason I became that Kid there was a cartoon in that (old dirty magazine). It was about a Kid in school during sex ed that asked the Teacher "What does all this have to do with getting laid?" He was made to write on the blackboard I am an Idiot over and over. At the time I thought it was alright to think the way I started, but now I really hate the way My mind has been working for the last forty years. Severe mental problems was another thing I learned in 1963, it is not the way You want to live Your life believe Me.

The funny thing as I look back now is, They stopped asking Me to do acid after that. I really do regret not reading that article that night too. I can bet it was a message directed straight at Me. I actually thought that (an old dirty magazine) was just a regular copy, until I tried to find it about eleven years ago. It was My own personal (an old dirty magazine) I know now.

I say Space Cadet, yes I became one. I stopped doing drugs I guess around thirteen years ago, now I just wish I could leave the beer alone too. I still smoke Marijauna every now and then, but I don't go looking for it anymore. When I get stoned I really do become a stupid Person, no shit. Especially if I have been drinking, then I can't shut up when I get high. It really is annoying to say the least.

I have two reasons for writing this book like I am doing. One, I hope it earns Me enough to build a home I can live out the rest of My life in along with enough cash to retire too. Mainly I hope I can shed some light on how bad drugs really are. And in doing so some Kids out there will understand that it is not alright to get as high as a kite. That is no way to be, wise up now. When I was told in school how they affected Your mind I thought I had a stronger mind than that, I was dead wrong. Learn from My mistakes Kids, take My word for it You do not want to destroy Your life like I did. Drugs are for Losers and that is a fact of life seriously. At this point I really don't care if I insult Someone here or not, I mean what I say, there are a lot of Losers on the Planet do not become one, really.

If You are reading this and My words hit home and You can see straight into what I am saying I truly feel pride right now, Live a good life and don't screw it up, please.

MY FINAL NOTES

In conclusion I have to say a few things. One is that I am still an innocent SOB. Quite often I still feel like a Boy, at the age of sixty two yes. Another is that I have seeked help in so many ways, Folks, I have gone to extremes. I must have contacted (a Person of fame) around fifty times, at least. I called the US Marshals so much when I first understood what happened They actually flat out told Me to stop calling Them. I even contacted the head of the FBI via email back then as well. I harassed (the owner of the old dirty magazine) to the point of ridiculousness. I have emailed (a large news show), the (a huge newspaper) and a few other news sources, nothing has helped. It seems that Nobody gives a shit about a Loser such as Me, but I refuse to give up.

As I stated I would love to make enough money off of this just to retire. I do not want to be the old Guy that has to continue to work until I am well into My seventies, but that is how it looks for Me as I see My life at the moment. The main thing I hope to accomplish by writing My life story is to awaken some People to how the World is. And a dream I have is to see Jerk #2 and Jerk #1 punished for Their crimes against My life. The saddest part about it is, I really doubt I have a chance at any of it.

With that said I wish You well and hope everything goes great for You in Your life. Sincerely, (nope, They say I can't say who I am. It might make People look bad. Meaning a couple of jerks).

ANOTHER ADD ON

I have to state here that I had to rewrite this as far as names being used and places as well. If You have read what I said you can understand why I really didn't want to do so. But the Publisher says I can be sued, Hell I hope they try. I am also supposed to make things up, why? I want it written in the manner I wrote it really. You have an angry SOB here and I deserve justice!

So, instead of rewriting the whole damn thing I figured it easier to scratch out a few things, You'll get the point.

If You did read this book about My sorry ass life I want to thank You.

Printed in the United States
by Baker & Taylor Publisher Services